# Labour Law in Iceland

# Labour Law in Iceland

## Third Edition

**Elín Blöndal**

This book was originally published as a monograph in the International Encyclopaedia of Laws/Labour Law and Industrial Relations.

Founding Editor: Roger Blanpain
General Editor: Frank Hendrickx
Volume Editor: Frank Hendrickx

*Published by:*
Kluwer Law International B.V.
PO Box 316
2400 AH Alphen aan den Rijn
The Netherlands
E-mail: international-sales@wolterskluwer.com
Website: lrus.wolterskluwer.com

*Sold and distributed in North, Central and South America by:*
Wolters Kluwer Legal & Regulatory U.S.
7201 McKinney Circle
Frederick, MD 21704
United States of America
Email: customer.service@wolterskluwer.com

*Sold and distributed in all other countries by:*
Air Business Subscriptions
Rockwood House
Haywards Heath
West Sussex
RH16 3DH
United Kingdom
Email: international-customerservice@wolterskluwer.com

DISCLAIMER: The material in this volume is in the nature of general comment only. It is not offered as advice on any particular matter and should not be taken as such. The editor and the contributing authors expressly disclaim all liability to any person with regard to anything done or omitted to be done, and with respect to the consequences of anything done or omitted to be done wholly or partly in reliance upon the whole or any part of the contents of this volume. No reader should act or refrain from acting on the basis of any matter contained in this volume without first obtaining professional advice regarding the particular facts and circumstances at issue. Any and all opinions expressed herein are those of the particular author and are not necessarily those of the editor or publisher of this volume.

*Printed on acid-free paper*

ISBN 978-94-035-0965-5

e-Book: ISBN 978-94-035-1004-0
web-PDF: ISBN 978-94-035-1052-1

Printed in the United Kingdom.

# The Author

 Elín Blöndal obtained a cand. jur. degree from the University of Iceland in 1992, a master's degree in Public International Law from the University of Leiden, Holland, in 1996 and a master's degree in Human Resource Management from the University of Iceland in 2017. Before she became the Chief Legal Counsel at the University of Iceland in 2013 she was a legal advisor at the Icelandic Parliament, Head of the Labour Office at the Ministry of Social Affairs, Head of Office at the Parliamentary Ombudsman, Professor at Bifröst University and chair of the Research Centre of Labour law at Bifröst University. Elín has written several publications, especially in the field of labour law, gender equality and social human rights. She has steered and participated in several committees and working groups as well as research projects at the national and international level in her field, e.g. the board of the Icelandic Labour Law Association, the consultant board of the Icelandic Lawyer's Association Law Review. She has also been a member of the European Labour Law Network (ELLN) and a judge in the Icelandic Labour Court.[1]

---

1. Katrín Elfa Gunnarsdóttir, student at the Faculty of Law, University of Iceland, assisted in the review of the book in 2018.

**The Author**

# Table of Contents

**Table of Contents**

**Table of Contents**

**Table of Contents**

# Chapter 5. Strikes, Lockouts and Other Legal Forms of Industrial Action

**Table of Contents**

# List of Abbreviations

| | |
|---|---|
| AOSH | The Administration of Occupational Safety and Health |
| ASÍ | The Icelandic Confederation of Labour |
| BHM | Confederation of Academic Workers |
| BSRB | The Confederation of Workers of the State and Communities |
| CAPS Act | The Act on Collective Agreements of Public Servants (94/1986) |
| EEA | The European Economic Area |
| ECHR | The European Convention on Human Rights |
| EFTA | The European Free Trade Association |
| EU | The European Union |
| GE Act | The Government Employment Act (70/1996) |
| ILO | The International Labour Organization |
| KÍ | The Teachers Union |
| LÍÚ | The Federation of Icelandic Fishing Vessel Owners |
| MPL Act | The Act on Maternity/Paternity Leave and Parental Leave (95/2000) |
| OECD | The Organisation for Economic Co-operation and Development |
| SA | The Confederation of Icelandic Employers |
| SAF | The Icelandic Travel Industry Association |
| SCMO | The State Conciliation and Mediation Officer |
| SFF | The Association of Financial Institutions in Iceland |
| SI | The Federation of Icelandic Industries |
| SVTH | The Federation of Trade and Services |
| SMEs | Small- and Medium-sized Enterprises |
| TEIA Act | The Act Respecting Labourers' Right to Advance Notice of Termination of Employment and to Wages on Account of Absence through Illness and Accidents (19/1979) |
| TUI Act | The Act on Trade Unions and Industrial Disputes |
| VMSS | Employers' Union of Cooperatives |
| VSÍ | The Icelandic Employers' Organization |

**List of Abbreviations**

WEHS Act    The Act on Working Conditions, Health and Safety in the
            Workplace (46/1980)
WTP Act     The Act on the Wage Earners' Terms of Service and Obligatory
            Pension Rights (55/1980)

# General Introduction

## Chapter 1. General Background

### §1. GEOGRAPHY, LOCATION, SIZE AND BOUNDARIES

*1.* Iceland is the second largest island in Europe and is located in the North Atlantic, east of Greenland and immediately south of the Arctic Circle. Iceland covers some 103,000 square kilometres and has a 4,988-kilometre coastline. Furthermore, Iceland controls 758,000 square kilometres of the North Atlantic Ocean which are within its economic zone. Iceland is one of the most volcanic regions in the world and has more land covered by glaciers than the whole of continental Europe, although the Gulf Stream keeps Iceland's climate milder than one would expect from an island near the Arctic Circle. For the most part Iceland's inhabitants live in the 7% of the island that is made up of fertile coastland, particularly in the south-west.

*2.* Iceland's population was 348,450 in January 2018, and some 8.9% thereof are foreigners. With only 3.4 inhabitants per square kilometre, Iceland is one of the least densely populated countries in Europe. The capital of Iceland is Reykjavik, and 63.8% of the population live in the greater Reykjavik area (Tables 1–3).

*3.* Icelanders are for the most parts descendants of Norwegian settlers and Celts from Ireland and Scotland. The national language is Icelandic, which is the Nordic languages the closest to the Old Norse language; it has remained relatively unchanged since the twelfth century.

*Table 1   Population and Annual Population Growth (2012–2017)*

|  | *2012* | *2013* | *2014* | *2015* | *2016* | *2017* |
|---|---|---|---|---|---|---|
| *Population* | 319,575 | 321,857 | 325,671 | 329,100 | 332,529 | 338,349 |
| *Population growth (%)* | 0.35 | 0.71 | 1.18 | 1.053 | 1.042 | 1.75 |

*Table 2   Population According to Gender (2012–2017)*

|         | 2012    | 2013    | 2014    | 2015    | 2016    | 2017    |
|---------|---------|---------|---------|---------|---------|---------|
| *Men*   | 160,364 | 161,438 | 163,318 | 165,186 | 167,270 | 171,033 |
| *Women* | 159,211 | 160,419 | 162,353 | 163,914 | 165,259 | 167,316 |

*Table 3   Foreign Population According to Gender (2012–2017)*

|         | 2012   | 2013   | 2014   | 2015   | 2016   | 2017   |
|---------|--------|--------|--------|--------|--------|--------|
| *Men*   | 12,190 | 12,339 | 13,140 | 14,134 | 15,707 | 18,552 |
| *Women* | 13,250 | 13,584 | 14,305 | 15,058 | 16,105 | 17,445 |

§2. THE POLITICAL SYSTEM

4. Iceland is a republic with a parliamentary government. The Icelandic Parliament, named *Althingi*, was established in 930 AD and was the foundation for the country's independence for the first centuries after its settlement. In 1262 Iceland came under the authority of the Norwegian crown, and in the late fourteenth century Iceland fell under the rule of Denmark when Norway and Denmark united under the Danish crown. Iceland remained a subject to the Danish crown until the twentieth century. In 1903 it received home rule and parliamentary government; in 1918 the Act of Union made Iceland a sovereign state and Iceland received full independence when the union with Denmark was dissolved in 1944. The Icelandic Constitution was promulgated the same year as the country received its independence, although large portions of it were unchanged from Iceland's first Constitution, brought about by the Danish in 1874. The Icelandic Constitution stood virtually unchanged until 1995 when important human rights provisions were amended, in accordance with several international human right treaties.

5. The Icelandic government consists of three branches: (1) legislative, (2) executive and (3) judicial. According to the Icelandic Constitution (Article 2), the President of Iceland and *Althingi* jointly exercise legislative power. However, in practice it is the parliament which holds the legislative power while the President gives parliamentary bills formal consent. It should be noted that the President has only on three occasions refused to consent a bill, in 2004, 2010 and 2011. *Althingi* is a legislative body of sixty-three members elected for a term of four years by popular vote. Anyone who is eligible to vote, with the exception of the President and the judges of the Supreme Court, can stand for Parliament. After every election, the President gives one of the parliamentary leaders of the political parties the authority to form a Cabinet. A Cabinet of ministers stays in power until the next general election or a new government is formed. The ministers sit in *Althingi*, but if they have not been elected, they do not have the right to vote in Parliament.

6. Following from Article 2 of the Constitution the President and other governmental authorities exercise executive power. Again, the executive power of the President is formal in nature since the President entrusts his authority to the ministers who then extend it to other bodies of the government. Each ministry consists of a central department with a number of ministerial agencies under its jurisdiction. According to Article 78 of the Constitution, varieties of public tasks are to be delegated to local municipalities. Each municipality is governed by an elected body of locally elected representatives. The extended range of tasks delegated is defined by the 2011 Local Government Act (138/2011).

7. The President, members of Parliament and local authorities are elected in general elections held every four years. In recent years Icelandic politics, both national and local, has been dominated by four major parties:

(1) the Independence Party (*Sjálfstædisflokkurinn*);
(2) the Social Democratic Alliance (*Samfylkingin*);
(3) the Progress Party (*Framsóknarflokkurinn*);
(4) the Left-Green Movement (*Vinstri hreyfingin grænt frambod*).

8. Regularly new parties and movements emerge and some of them have successfully had their representatives elected to the Parliament, although traditionally they have not enjoyed long-term success.

9. According to the Constitution (Article 2), judges exercise judicial power. The 2016 Act on Courts (50/2016) is the main Act on the organization of the judiciary. The Icelandic judicial court system was constructed on two levels until 1 January 2018 when a new court level was introduced, replacing the former two tiers with a three-tier system. The new court is called the Court of Appeal (*Landsréttur*) and is a court of second instance, situated between the District Court and the Supreme Court. The introduction of the Court of Appeal was part of a major restructuring of the Icelandic justice system. All court actions in Iceland commence in the District Courts (*Héraðsdómstólar*), which are eight in number and located around the country. The District Courts have jurisdiction in civil as well as criminal cases. The conclusion of a District Court can be appealed to the Court of Appeal, provided specific conditions for appeal are satisfied. In special cases, and after receiving the permission of the Supreme Court, it will be possible to refer the conclusion of the Court of Appeal to the Supreme Court, but in most instances the judgment of the Court of Appeal will be the final resolution in the case. There are a total of sixty-four judges in Iceland, forty-two of whom preside over the eight District Courts. The Court of Appeal has fifteen judges and the Supreme Court has seven. In addition, there are two Special Courts: (1) the Labour Court (*Félagsdómur*), which deals with trade union matters and industrial disputes, and (2) the Court of Impeachment (*Landsdómur*), which has competence if Ministers, in pursuance of their official tasks, are impeached. Dozens of cases are brought before the Labour Court each year, but a decision to convene the Court of Impeachment was made for the first time in September 2010.

§3.  VITAL STATISTICS

## I.  Employment

10. Through the centuries Iceland has been a relatively poor country whose economy was mainly based on fragile agriculture. Until 1975 almost two-thirds of the labour force was employed in agriculture. The Icelandic economy has for a long time been largely based on the utilization of natural resources, such as in the fisheries, agriculture and energy industries. In recent years, the diversity of the business sector has expanded in parallel with rapid technological progress, focusing on innovation and creative industries, and the rapid growth of tourism.

11. Work participation in Iceland has in recent years been among the highest in The Organisation for Economic Co-operation and Development (OECD) countries, and both genders are in general active in the labour market. The participation rate of women has been very high by international comparison. Additionally Icelanders tend to work long hours and it is not uncommon for people to have more than one job. A low unemployment rate has been one of the main characteristics of the Icelandic labour market. It however reached a peak in the year 2009 as a result of the economic crisis in the autumn of 2008 but has decreased considerably since then. In 2017 the registered unemployment rate was on average 2.8% (Table 4).

*Table 4   Work Participation Rate and Unemployment Rate According to Gender (%) (2011–2018)*

|            | 2011 | 2012 | 2013 | 2014 | 2015 | 2016 | 2017 |
|------------|------|------|------|------|------|------|------|
| **Working** |      |      |      |      |      |      |      |
| *Total*    | 80.5 | 80.5 | 81.4 | 81.5 | 82.5 | 83.6 | 82.6 |
| *Men*      | 83.7 | 83.1 | 84.2 | 84.7 | 85.7 | 87.4 | 86.2 |
| *Women*    | 77.1 | 77.7 | 78.5 | 78.2 | 79.3 | 79.6 | 78.7 |
| **Unemployed** |  |      |      |      |      |      |      |
| *Total*    | 7.1  | 6.0  | 5.4  | 5.0  | 4.0  | 3.0  | 2.8  |
| *Men*      | 7.8  | 6.4  | 5.7  | 5.1  | 3.9  | 2.9  | 2.8  |
| *Women*    | 6.2  | 5.7  | 5.1  | 4.9  | 4.1  | 3.1  | 2.7  |

12. Although there is a very high work participation rate among women in Iceland, women are more likely than men to work part-time. In 2016, 15% of men was employed part-time (<35 hours per week) but 35% of women was part-time employed.

13. As stated above, the work participation rate in Iceland is among the highest in the world and as seen in Table 5 the rate is generally high in all age groups.

18

*Table 5   Work Participation Rate According to Age (%) (2011–2017)*

|  | 2011 | 2012 | 2013 | 2014 | 2015 | 2016 | 2017 |
|---|---|---|---|---|---|---|---|
| *16–24 years* | 74.1 | 76.3 | 78.9 | 77.5 | 79.5 | 82.5 | 81.7 |
| *25–54 years* | 89.1 | 89.2 | 89.7 | 89.6 | 90.7 | 91.9 | 91.3 |
| *55–74 years* | 65.3 | 64.2 | 65.4 | 67.2 | 68.0 | 67.7 | 65.8 |

## II.  Employment in Different Industries

*14.*  As stated in paragraph 10 most of the Icelandic labour force worked in agriculture until late in the last century. Since Iceland won sovereignty over the fishing grounds around the island, fishery has been one of the fundamental industries in Iceland and the main source of foreign exchange earnings. With the advent of other industries in the last few decades both the market share and the importance of the fishing industry has decreased. However, after the financial crisis and the collapse of the financial system in 2008, the importance of the fishery has risen again and fish are widely considered the most important export product in Iceland. The importance of the fishing industry is, however, not reflected in the number of jobs the industry creates in Iceland as seen in Table 6. According to statistics, the most populated industry in Iceland is the retail and wholesale industry, followed by health services and social work. The importance of the hotels and restaurants industry, which comes third, has increased considerably in recent years, due to the growing tourism in Iceland.

*15.*  As seen in Table 6, the gender ratio in different industries is quite uneven. Industries like health services and social work as well as education are primarily female dominated, while industries like fishery, construction, manufacturing as well as electricity and water supply are male dominated.

*Table 6   Industry Participation According to Gender (2011–2017)*

|  | 2011 | 2012 | 2013 | 2014 | 2015 | 2016 | 2017 |
|---|---|---|---|---|---|---|---|
| **Employed persons** |  |  |  |  |  |  |  |
| *Total* | 163,706 | 166,587 | 170,634 | 174,640 | 179,941 | 188,466 | 197,088 |
| *Men* | 83,971 | 85,878 | 88,202 | 90,266 | 93,346 | 98,794 | 104,403 |
| *Women* | 79,735 | 80,709 | 82,432 | 84,374 | 86.594 | 89.672 | 92.685 |
| **Agriculture** |  |  |  |  |  |  |  |
| *Total* | 3.688 | 3.732 | 3.763 | 3.754 | 3.820 | 3.825 | 3.763 |

|  | 2011 | 2012 | 2013 | 2014 | 2015 | 2016 | 2017 |
|---|---|---|---|---|---|---|---|
| Men | 2.456 | 2.480 | 2.513 | 2.502 | 2.536 | 2.539 | 1.286 |
| Women | 1.232 | 1.252 | 1.251 | 1.253 | 1.284 | 2.495 | 1.268 |
| **Fishing** | | | | | | | |
| Total | 4.416 | 4.367 | 4.218 | 3.933 | 3.807 | 3.601 | 3.290 |
| Men | 4.082 | 4.025 | 3.876 | 3.552 | 3.476 | 3.295 | 3.011 |
| Women | 334 | 342 | 342 | 382 | 332 | 306 | 279 |
| **Fish processing** | | | | | | | |
| Total | 5.538 | 5.842 | 6.153 | 6.210 | 6.105 | 6.029 | 5.660 |
| Men | 3.017 | 3.183 | 3.352 | 3.458 | 3.373 | 3.368 | 3.169 |
| Women | 2.520 | 2.660 | 2.800 | 2.752 | 2.732 | 2.661 | 2.491 |
| **Manufacturing except fish processing** | | | | | | | |
| Total | 15.804 | 16.088 | 16.248 | 16.485 | 16.773 | 17.309 | 17.469 |
| Men | 11.317 | 11.531 | 11.649 | 11.833 | 12.082 | 12.429 | 12.539 |
| Women | 4.488 | 4.556 | 4.600 | 4.652 | 4.691 | 4.880 | 4.930 |
| **Electricity and water supply** | | | | | | | |
| Total | 2.469 | 2.465 | 2.468 | 2.511 | 2.568 | 2.597 | 2.667 |
| Men | 1.910 | 1.911 | 1.900 | 1.937 | 1.969 | 1.987 | 2.031 |
| Women | 559 | 554 | 568 | 574 | 600 | 610 | 636 |
| **Construction** | | | | | | | |
| Total | 8.660 | 8.577 | 9.112 | 9.743 | 10.612 | 12.158 | 14.035 |
| Men | 8.087 | 8.005 | 8.502 | 9.078 | 9.906 | 11.364 | 13.164 |
| Women | 573 | 572 | 610 | 665 | 705 | 793 | 871 |
| **Wholesale and retail trade** | | | | | | | |
| Total | 23.075 | 23.796 | 24.139 | 24.645 | 25.285 | 26.524 | 27.862 |
| Men | 12.429 | 13.020 | 13.256 | 13.554 | 13.932 | 14.673 | 15.631 |
| Women | 10.646 | 10.777 | 10.883 | 11.091 | 11.353 | 11.852 | 12.232 |
| **Hotels and restaurants** | | | | | | | |
| Total | 9.465 | 10.353 | 11.401 | 12.482 | 14.155 | 16.195 | 17.548 |
| Men | 4.030 | 4.448 | 4.914 | 5.373 | 6.147 | 7.109 | 7.881 |
| Women | 5.435 | 5.906 | 6.486 | 7.109 | 8.008 | 9.087 | 9.667 |

|                                          | 2011   | 2012   | 2013   | 2014   | 2015   | 2016   | 2017   |
|------------------------------------------|--------|--------|--------|--------|--------|--------|--------|
| **Transport and communication**          |        |        |        |        |        |        |        |
| *Total*                                  | 9.693  | 9.985  | 10.416 | 10.892 | 11.572 | 13.188 | 14.594 |
| *Men*                                    | 6.498  | 6.708  | 7.001  | 7.244  | 7.674  | 8.637  | 9.428  |
| *Women*                                  | 3.196  | 3.277  | 3.416  | 3.648  | 3.898  | 4.551  | 5.166  |
| **Financial intermediation**             |        |        |        |        |        |        |        |
| *Total*                                  | 7.218  | 7.115  | 6.905  | 6.716  | 6.459  | 6.404  | 6.305  |
| *Men*                                    | 2.921  | 2.914  | 2.849  | 2.783  | 2.745  | 2.787  | 2.748  |
| *Women*                                  | 4.297  | 4.201  | 4.056  | 3.933  | 3.715  | 3.617  | 3.556  |
| **Public administration**                |        |        |        |        |        |        |        |
| *Total*                                  | 14.442 | 14.266 | 14.266 | 14.242 | 14.117 | 13.936 | 14.409 |
| *Men*                                    | 7.273  | 7.150  | 7.068  | 6.968  | 6.852  | 6.736  | 6.804  |
| *Women*                                  | 7.169  | 7.116  | 7.198  | 7.274  | 7.264  | 7.199  | 7.605  |
| **Education**                            |        |        |        |        |        |        |        |
| *Total*                                  | 20.445 | 20.521 | 20.894 | 21.357 | 21.777 | 21.691 | 21.525 |
| *Men*                                    | 4.776  | 4.805  | 4.903  | 5.004  | 5.048  | 5.021  | 4.946  |
| *Women*                                  | 15.669 | 15.716 | 15.992 | 16.353 | 16.729 | 16.670 | 16.579 |
| **Health services and social work**      |        |        |        |        |        |        |        |
| *Total*                                  | 20.672 | 20.811 | 21.180 | 21.624 | 22.242 | 22.194 | 22.740 |
| *Men*                                    | 4.241  | 4.385  | 4.551  | 4.670  | 4.838  | 4.693  | 4.804  |
| *Women*                                  | 16.431 | 16.425 | 16.629 | 16.954 | 17.404 | 17.501 | 17.937 |

§4. UNDERLYING SOCIAL AND CULTURAL VALUES OF SOCIETY

*16.* Iceland is a welfare state and as such much emphasis has been placed on social welfare and social security. Unemployment benefits and measures aimed at securing jobs are one of the highest expenditures in the national budget. National legislation ensures all citizens a guaranteed income, in the form of disability compensation, unemployment benefits, social security or pensions for those not active in the labour market. Certain rights like freedom of assembly and association are constitutionally protected as well as there being a ban on discrimination. In recent years, increased weight has been put on the issue of gender equality and the focus has been on equal salaries and equal opportunity in the labour market.

# Chapter 2. Definitions and Notions

§1. DISTINCTION BETWEEN LABOUR LAW (INDUSTRIAL RELATIONS) AND OTHER
BRANCHES OF LAW, ESPECIALLY SOCIAL SECURITY LAW

*17.* Icelandic social legislation comprises labour law on the one hand, including
equality in the labour market as well as health and safety at the workplace, and
social security law on the other. The Nordic model on which the Icelandic labour
system is built emphasizes social welfare and social security. This close-knit relationship between labour law and social security law can therefore make it difficult
in some cases to distinguish between the two branches. In recent years factors such
as job satisfaction, equal rights and opportunities as well as a good work/life balance have become increasingly important.

## I. Social Security Law

*18.* Social security legislation in Iceland provides a certain statutory minimum
social insurance coverage. Everyone who has been a legal resident in Iceland for a
certain period of time automatically becomes a member of the Icelandic social
insurance system, regardless of nationality. The Icelandic social security system
covers:

– pension insurance;
– health insurance;
– occupational injury insurance;
– unemployment insurance;
– family benefits (child allowance).

*19.* Legislation provides certain conditions which must be met to become
entitled to benefits, which include conditions regarding age, disability and time of
residence. Income and family circumstances can also have an influence on entitlement.

*20.* The Social Insurance Administration (*Tryggingastofnun*) is a governmental
service institution seeing, e.g., to the payment of pension insurance and social assistance. The Directorate of Labour (*Vinnumálastofnun*) is responsible for and admin-
isters unemployment insurance. Family benefits are administered by the Directorate
of Internal Revenue (*Fjársýsla ríkisins*).

*21.* Social insurance in Iceland is financed by the State Treasury (*Ríkissjódur*).
Individuals do not pay special premiums for their social insurance; instead, employers pay premiums to the State Treasury on all paid wages.

## II. Labour Law

22. In general, the term 'labour law' covers all legislation and rules regarding regulations of the labour market and the relationship between employers and employees. Furthermore, the term is considered to cover statutes regarding the work environment.

23. In practice, Icelandic labour law is typically divided into two branches: (1) collective labour law and (2) individual labour law. Collective labour law contains the legal rules which regulate collective agreements, and individual labour law contains the legal rules which apply to the relationship and contracts between employers and employees. However, the two sub-branches of labour law overlap in some cases, which can make it quite challenging to draw a clear distinction between the two.

24. The term labour law has been considered to apply to any labour or work done in a position of subordination, i.e., work done under the authority and control of an employer. Thus, self-employed individuals do not in principle fall under labour rules and legislation and therefore do not enjoy the full protection and benefits that social legislation has to offer.

§2. DEFINITIONS OF LABOUR LAW AND OF THE CONCEPTS WHICH ARE MOST FREQUENTLY USED

## I. The Employment Relationship

25. No legislative definition of the term 'employment relationship' exists in Iceland but the definition has evolved through custom and judicial decisions. Commonly, employment relationships are based on an employment contract, which is a contract between an employer and an employee, where the employee binds himself to work for the employer, under his control and responsibility in return for wages. The customary definition of an employment contract is a contract between the employer and the employee, where the employee engages himself to work for the employer, under his supervision and on his responsibility in return for wages. In general there are no legal stipulations requiring the contract to be in writing and a verbal contract is considered just as valid as a written one, according to judicial precedent. A valid employment contract can even be established without any formal relation between the parties. It should, however, be pointed out that under collective agreements, if an employee is hired for longer period than one month and on the average for more than eight hours a week, the employer has the duty to provide the employee with a written employment contract or a letter of engagement.

26. Numerous cases have gone before the Supreme Court involving disputes over the status of employment and whether an employment relationship had been established. The definition of the parties and even their intention has not proven to be decisive factors, but rather the nature of their relationship. In the absence of an

23

employment contract the courts look at different factors to determine whether an employment relationship has been formed or not. These are factors like the duration and continuity of the task, separation from general operations, wage-related expenses, facilities, provision of tools and materials, the responsibility and risk of the task in question, the relationship between the negotiating parties, union affiliation, type of remuneration, sick days, whether the work is carried out personally, independence, vacation pay, tax payments, work supervision and work hours.

*27.* Even though a formal employment contract is not a requirement in forming an employment relationship, it is the most common means of establishing one and most employers use formal written employment contracts in all their hirings. In some instances legislation stipulates requirements for a written employment contract, like the 1985 Seamen Act (35/1985), the 2011 Local Government Act, the 2002 Foreign Nationals' Right to Work Act (97/2002) and the 2005 Act on Temporary-work Agencies (139/2005) (*see* paragraphs 80–86 below).

## II. Employee

*28.* No general statutory definition of the term 'employee' exists in Iceland. Consequently, the term has been developed by the courts and defined as a person who is employed by and under the supervision of another person, and receives taxable salary or remuneration for his work. However, there are a few examples of the term being defined in the meaning of some Acts, like the 2006 Unemployment Insurance Act (54/2006), the 1980 Act on Working Conditions, Health and Safety in the Workplace (WEHS) Act (46/1980) and the 1987 Act on Withholding Taxes (45/1987). The term 'employee' under Icelandic labour law is not definite since it is evaluated every time whether the person concerned is to be considered as an employee or self-employed. In Iceland, existing legislation and collective agreements are, in principle, based on the division of labour between two groups: (1) employees, that is those who are employed, and (2) self-employed persons who work independently. The legal status of self-employed persons is quite different from that of employees, since they are not entitled to the same rights and benefits as employees, including minimum wages, sick days and paid vacation, terms of annulment and unemployment benefits. Legislation concerning employee's rights is in general unwavering and meant to guarantee certain rights and benefits. It is therefore compulsory, and it is not possible to negotiate specific legal employee rights away by contract. These provisions do not in general cover self-employed persons. When dealing with uncommon forms of employment, the question would therefore be whether the relevant individual should be considered an employee or a self-employed person. As regards 'new forms of employment' some forms are uncommon on the Icelandic labour market, such as the voucher systems (employment relationships based on vouchers or cheques the requestor of a service can acquire from a third party), job sharing (a single employer hires a group of workers to jointly fill a specific job, who perform the same work on a rotational basis within the same company) and specific employment statutes (combining elements of traditional dependent employment and self-employment). Other forms are more common, such as crowd employment (virtual platforms matching buyers and sellers of services), interim management (when a worker is temporarily hired by an employer, often to work on a specific project) and ICT-based, mobile work (the employment terms are characterized by the worker, who either works from home, at the client's premises, on the road, etc.). Causal work (an employment relationship which does not oblige the employer to provide the employee with regular work) is the only form of employment that has caused problems in practice, mainly because there has been a tendency by employers to avoid the rule of minimum wage under collective agreements.

## III. Employer

29.    There is no general statutory definition of the term 'employer' in Iceland, but there are examples of the term being defined in the meaning of some Acts, like the 1980 WEHS Act. In the field of labour law, the term employer has been defined as the party to an employment relationship that purchases work, whether being an individual, company, limited company, institution, municipality or the state.

## Chapter 3. Historical Background

*30.* Iceland was a Danish colony until 1918, and Icelandic labour legislation is in many ways built on the Danish model. A modern labour market was not established in Iceland until the turn of the twentieth century at the same time as the first trade unions were established. In 1901 the first law on the payment of wages entered into force in Iceland, but the law was intended to prevent wages being paid in goods, which was common at that time. The Icelandic Confederation of Labour (ASÍ) was established in 1916 and is still today the largest federation of workers in Iceland, with the majority of trade unions in the private sector. Employers formed their own organizations in response to the trade unions, and in 1934 the Confederation of Icelandic Employers (VSÍ, now SA) was established. In these initial years, limited legislation led to severe industrial disputes with much participation from political parties, which had great influence on the labour movement.

*31.* In 1938 the first comprehensive legislation regarding the labour market, the Act on Trade Unions and Industrial Disputes ((TUI) Act, 80/1938)), was passed by the Icelandic Parliament and marked the beginning of a new era in Icelandic labour rights. The Act set out the rules in industrial disputes, rules on collective agreements, shop stewards, strikes and lockouts, the foundation of and open admittance to trade unions as well as conciliation in industrial disputes. The Act furthermore stipulated the establishment of the Labour Court (Félagsdómur), a special court addressing labour affairs. The Act is still valid although it has been revised, and it is the foundation of industrial relations in Iceland.

# Chapter 4. Role of Government Institutions in the Shaping and Administration of Labour and Industrial Relations Policy

*32.* Icelandic trade unions have for a long time had a strong position on the Icelandic labour market and for a long time it has proved difficult for the labour movement to agree on an integrated policy on pay. In 1990 this changed when the National Social Pacts (*thjóðarsáttarsamningarnir*) were signed. These agreements, which were negotiated between ASÍ and SA, placed the emphasis on matters other than direct pay increases and thereby opened a new phase in the resolution of pay disputes. Since then this policy has been followed, and thus a general pay policy has been formulated aiming to control inflation and achieve stability in economic affairs.

*33.* The state does not have any administrative authority to intervene in wage negotiations, and collective agreements are not subject to approval by ministerial order. In spite of this the government nowadays plays a considerable role in the resolution of wage disputes, the aim being to make measures of wage restraint more acceptable in the context of broader political exchange controlled by the state. This kind of support from the government and legislature has been introduced by a declaration from the government, made in connection with the conclusion of collective agreements, and has covered economic measures as well as social issues of various kinds, such as housing policy, unemployment insurance, pensions and taxation (often named 'social packages'). Some legislation in the public welfare area, like the 2006 Unemployment Insurance Act (54/2006), may be traced back to these measures. As mentioned, this would in general be made by a declaration from the government, but there are also examples of tripartite agreements, made between the government and the main social partners, in connection with the conclusion of collective agreements. Following the 2008 financial crises, the so-called Stability Pact was thus agreed on, the main objective being to promote economic recovery following the financial crisis. Under the Pact the social partners joined forces to remove labour market uncertainty, by concluding collective bargaining agreements valid until the end of November 2010, which emphasized improving the situation of the lowest income groups. The Stability Pact covered, e.g., work projects to encourage increased employment. In order to set a new and sustainable path for increases in wages, the representatives of employees and employers in Iceland signed an agreement in early 2016 modelled after Nordic wage agreements structure. This agreement, which has been referred to as SALEK (Samstarf um launaupplýsingar og efnahagsforsendur kjarasamninga), stipulated that wage cost increases should not exceed 32% in the period of 2013–2018. The goal is to increase purchasing power on the basis of low inflation, low interest rates and stable exchange rates. The agreement has, however, been a matter of controversy among labour unions, and a number of labour union leaders, particularly those who operate in the private market, have criticized it heavily. Furthermore, evidence is mounting up that the agreement has not held.

*34.* In Iceland there is a strong tradition of tripartite consultation with the social partners when it comes to matters of labour market issues as well as economic and social policies. Some government institutions play a large role in the Icelandic labour market. The Ministry of Welfare is in charge of labour legislation, and a number of public institutions deal with labour market issues, such as the Directorate of Labour, the Administration of Occupational Safety and Health (AOSH) (*Vinnueftirlit ríkisins*) and the Centre for Gender Equality (*Jafnréttisstofa*). Furthermore, the government can take part in negotiation process between the parties on the labour market through the State Conciliation and Mediation Officer (SCMO) (*Ríkissáttasemjari*) which acts as an independent and impartial mediator between the disputing parties. In extreme cases where it is considered that an industrial dispute will have extremely serious consequences, the government can intervene by appointing a special conciliation committee to work towards the resolution of the dispute.

## §1. The Directorate of Labour

*35.* The Directorate of Labour manages the employment service in Iceland as well as the daily work of the Unemployment Benefit Fund, the Wage Guarantee Fund, the Childbirth Leave Fund and payments to parents of children with long-term illnesses. The Directorate works according to the 2006 Act on Labour Market Affairs (55/2006) and the 2006 Act on Unemployment Insurance (54/2006), as well as related regulations. The main tasks of the Directorate are to supervise the employment service centres and coordinate their activities, take care of funds, accounts and daily expedition for the Unemployment Insurance Fund (*Atvinnuleysistryggingasjódur*), administer the daily expedition of the Vocational board of the Ministry of Welfare and give work permits under the mandate of the Ministry of Welfare. Furthermore, the Directorate of Labour has to gather information on the employment situation in Iceland, unemployment and employment prospects as well as monitoring the composition of the workforce.

## §2. The Administration of Occupational Safety and Health

*36.* AOSH is an independent institution under the Ministry of Welfare which works according to the 1980 WEHS Act, as well as related regulations covering workplaces on land with a staff of one or more persons. Its role is to prevent accidents and health damage in the workplace. The AOSH's main task is enforcing legislation regarding workplace conditions. Its tasks also include devising and execution of courses regarding health and safety in the workplace as well as inspection and supervision of workplace machinery and other conditions to ensure that the health and safety legislation and regulations are being followed in workplaces. Furthermore, the AOSH is in charge of reviewing and measuring noise, pollution and indoor air in Icelandic workplaces.

### §3. THE STATE CONCILIATION AND MEDIATION OFFICER

*37.* SCMO is appointed by the Minister of Welfare for a term of five years at a time. The SCMO works on the basis of the TUI Act and related regulations. In accordance with law, special effort is made to ensure that the SCMO's attitude is such that he may be regarded as impartial in matters involving employees and employers. The role of the SCMO is to work for conciliation in industrial disputes between employees and their unions, on the one hand, and employers and their associations on the other. He also monitors the situation and outlook in the economy and the employment market throughout the country and keeps abreast of the wages and terms situation and matters which might cause disputes in relations between employers' associations and trade unions. Furthermore, the officer keeps a register of valid collective agreements, and employees' and employers' organizations as well, and non-affiliated employers are obliged to send him copies of all collective agreements they conclude as soon as they are signed.

## Chapter 5. Sources of Labour Law

*38.* Historically, Icelandic labour law has mainly consisted of general legislation, court decisions and collective agreements as well as individual agreements. In recent years, amendments to the Constitution have made some of its articles relevant to the field of labour law. As a member of various international organizations, such as the United Nations, the International Labour Organization (ILO) and OECD, Iceland has an increasing number of international obligations in the labour field. The most influential of Iceland's international commitments is, however, without a doubt the European Economic Area (EEA) agreement (*see* further in paragraphs 45 and 46). Iceland furthermore ratified the European Social Charter by a Parliamentary Act in 1976. The sources of Icelandic labour law are therefore both national and international in nature. However, in accordance with the Icelandic Constitution, international conventions are not self-executing, and ratification only entails an obligation on the part of the state to adapt its legislation if necessary. Hence, the provisions of international conventions do not serve as a source of law in Iceland unless they have been implemented in national legislation.

### §1. Constitution

*39.* The Icelandic Constitution did not have any provisions relating to labour law until 1995 when the human rights section was reviewed and reworded to conform with the international agreements of which Iceland is a signatory. The amendments made to the Constitution contain a few provisions regarding labour law. Article 74 stipulates the freedom of assembly, association and peaceful demonstration. Nevertheless, these rights are not totally unconditional; thus a lawful purpose is a requirement as well as that the rights may not jeopardize public safety. The provision regarding freedom of association has a particular importance since it secures the right of existence and formation of unions (*see* further in paragraph 248). Article 75 stipulates that every citizen is free to choose his own profession. However, this freedom can be limited by legislation if public interest so demands and professions that are unlawful are not protected by the article. According to paragraph 2 of the same article the duty is put on the legislator to ensure citizens' right to negotiate their wages and other work-related benefits with general legislation. Finally, Article 76 states that national law shall include provisions that guarantee citizens' rights to social security and unemployment benefits. In addition Article 65 of the Constitution stipulates equal rights, regardless of gender, race, religious preferences, etc. This constitutional ban on discrimination has a strong relation to Icelandic labour law and the labour market as well as being the foundation of equal rights legislation in Iceland.

### §2. Acts of the Legislature and Judge-Made Law

*40.* No complete legislation regarding labour and social affairs exists in Iceland, but current legislation covers various aspects of labour and social law. Generally the legislation lays down the basic principles governing workers' rights and obligations, i.e., the laws state minimum rights, and agreements made on the basis of more restricted rights are therefore void.

*41.* As mentioned earlier, the fundamental legislation regarding the Icelandic labour market is the 1938 TUI Act, with subsequent amendments. The Act sets out the rules and conciliation in industrial disputes, rules on collective agreements, shop stewards, strikes and lockouts as well as ensuring the foundation and operation of trade unions. Furthermore, the Act is the foundation of the Labour Court which addresses labour disputes regarding issues covered by the Act.

*42.* The 1980 WEHS Act is a general statute about working conditions. The purpose of the Act is to ensure a safe and healthy working environment as well as ensuring such conditions within the workplace that it is possible to resolve safety and health problems in accordance with Acts and regulations.

*43.* Numerous other Acts and administrative actions (administrative regulations/ statutory instruments) which affect the conditions on the labour market are in place. These apply to specific areas of the labour market, regarding such matters as working hours, holidays, parental leave and gender equality, for example.

*44.* Even though legislation must be considered the principal source of labour law in Iceland, judge-made law can in some cases have equal value. The decisions made by the Labour Court as well as the Supreme Court have played an important role in the development of labour law. This applies particularly in areas where the statute is deficient. For example, the legal definition of an employment relationship has evolved through custom and judicial decisions and no legislative definition exists in current legislation. It has to be kept in mind, though, that with more extensive legislation the significance of judge-made law subsides, although it still retains its value when it comes to interpretation of existing legislation.

§3. THE EUROPEAN ECONOMIC AREA

*45.* Iceland has been a member of the EEA since its inception in 1994 and numerous regulations and directives by the European Union (EU) have become a part of the EEA agreement. In accordance with the EEA agreement Iceland is required to implement EU instruments (regulations/directives) that are within the scope of the agreement. Furthermore, these provisions shall have priority effects in the case of conflict with domestic law, cf. Protocol 35 to the EEA agreement.

*46.* Those regulations and directives relating to the labour market and industrial relations have generated much development in Icelandic labour affairs and have been included in laws and collective agreements. The subjects of EU directives/ regulations implemented into Icelandic labour law can be divided into three main categories. First they relate directly to the labour market and the relationship between employers and employees. Issues covered by this category are for example the rights of employees in the case of collective redundancies or transfers of under-takings, salary responsibility in the case of bankruptcy and the employees' right to have the terms of employment in writing. The second category relates to working conditions and the protection of employees from a hazardous environment in the workplace. This includes maximum working hours during specific periods as well as minimum rest periods. This category also relates to rules regarding work facili-ties, security labelling and protection gear. Furthermore, rules about the rights of pregnant women and women who are nursing as well work protection regarding minors are covered by this category. The third and final category comprises rules regarding gender equality, and the wide spectrum of rules covered in this category focuses on equality in all areas of the labour market.

§4. COLLECTIVE AGREEMENTS

*47.* The Icelandic labour system is mainly based on collective agreements, and the vast majority of wage earners in Iceland, approximately 85%, are unionized. As mentioned above, labour legislation in Iceland lays down certain minimum rights, thus making it possible for labour unions and employers to agree on more favour-able solutions regarding wages as well as other benefits through collective bargain-ing.

*48.* The 1938 TUI Act governs collective bargaining in Iceland and empowers trade unions to negotiate agreements with employers concerning wages and other terms of employment of their members. The 1986 Act on Collective Agreements of Public Servants (CAPS Act, 94/1986) applies to the public sector.

*49.* Collective agreements cover all workers in the relevant occupations in the geographical area to which each agreement applies. On the basis of the 1980 Act on the Wage Earners' Terms of Service and Obligatory Pension Rights (WTP Act, 55/1980), the agreements not only apply to union members affiliated to a particular agreement but also to wages and the other terms of all wage earners in the relevant occupations in the area covered by the agreements. Thus, collective agreements serve for all purposes as compulsory law and the rights stipulated in such agree-ments are legally binding as minimum rights, when applicable. The binding effect of collective agreements is enforceable by the Labour Court.

*50.* The general content of collective agreements can be divided into three main categories. The first category stipulates rates of pay depending on various factors, divided into daytime and overtime rates, and the influence of other factors such as type of work, age, work experience. It furthermore includes provisions on meal and coffee breaks and minimum hours of daily and weekly rest. The second category relates to holiday payments, health and safety at the workplace, payments in cases of sickness and work-related accidents, working clothes, trade union and pension fund fees, rules on notice of dismissal, selection and duties of trade union represen-tatives, etc. The third and final category stipulates the term of the agreement and in some cases dispute resolution of the negotiating parties and how to deal with changes that occur in underlying economic factors, such as inflation, which affect the expected outcome of real wages during the validity of the agreement.

*51.* The most common type of collective agreements made in Iceland are general collective agreements (*almennir kjarasamningar/heildarkjarasamningar*), usually negotiated by the national confederations, in most cases ASÍ and SA, on behalf of several or all of their member unions. General collective agreements are in several occupational sectors supplemented with so-called special agreements (*sérkjarasamningar*) negotiated by trade unions at the local level on various issues such as shift work arrangements. The third category, workplace agreements (*vinnustaðasamningar*) have been negotiated for large industrial companies such as aluminium corporations and hydroelectric power plant projects. In those cases agreements can be negotiated on behalf of a number of trade unions belonging to different occupational sectors and national federations. In addition, enterprise agreements (*fyrirtækjasamningar*) are in general made between one national association of trade unions and a particular company. These collective agreements cover one or more member unions within the national association. They are either independent or refer to the relevant collective agreement on certain matters.

*52.* Since 1997 all general collective agreements have included a chapter called company-related parts of collective agreements (*fyrirtækjatháttur kjarasamninga*). These concern the alignment of the collective agreement to the requirements of the workplace and enhance the cooperation of employees and management at the workplace. See further the description of the different types of collective agreements in paragraphs 329–332.

§5.  THE INDIVIDUAL EMPLOYMENT CONTRACT

*53.* The general rule regarding contracts is that the parties have the freedom to conclude contracts by their own preference containing subjects in accordance with their own wishes. Nevertheless the freedom to conclude employment contracts is limited through the means of statutory law and collective agreements which cannot be deviated from the detriment of the employee. As previously described, it is a fundamental rule in Icelandic labour law that legislative provisions as well as collective agreements are compulsory minimum rights that cannot be waived. Such breach of law or collective agreement would render the employment contract null and void in whole or in part. If there is no applicable statute or collective agreement relating to the contract in question, the parties are free to conclude a contract of employment in accordance with their own preferences.

§6. Relationship (Hierarchical Order) Between the Different Sources
    of Labour Law

*54.* In accordance to what has been written above a certain hierarchy of sources
has been established. Legislation and statutes that stipulate minimum rights are non-
negotiable and cannot be deviated from. Therefore, compulsory legal rules would
be at the top of the hierarchy and the Constitution is the highest ranking source of
law. Rules originating from the EEA agreement which have been implemented into
Icelandic legislation have in principle the same status as domestic legislation, but in
the case of a conflict between the two the EEA rules take precedence.

*55.* In practice, collective agreements have a strong resemblance to legal rules
as well as a similar effect. However, collective agreements cannot include stipulations that deviate from legal rules in a way unfavourable to the employee. However,
there can be conflict between different types of agreements which makes it necessary to set up a hierarchical order. In those cases general agreements would take precedence over special agreements, enterprise agreements or workplace agreements,
if the effect of the conflict in question reduced the employee's rights.

*56.* The individual employment contract establishes certain rights for the
employee that can be enforceable through the courts. However, it is generally considered to be a legal source of secondary importance in Icelandic labour law, hence
its provisions cannot deviate from stipulations in legislation or collective
agreements.

# Chapter 6. International Private Labour Law

*57.* The 2000 Act on Private International Contract Law (43/2000) implemented the rules of the Rome Convention on the law applicable to contractual obligations (1980). The Act applies to choice of law issues involving contractual obligations. The principal rule is that a contract is governed by the law chosen by the parties. If the law applicable to the contract has not been chosen, the contract is governed by the law of the country to which it is most closely connected. The choice of law of the parties of an individual employment contract should not have the result of depriving the employee of the protection afforded to him/her by the mandatory rules of the law which would be applicable in the absence of that choice. If there is no express selection, an employment contract is governed by the law of the country in which the employee habitually carries out his work in performance of the contract, even if he is temporarily employed in another country, or if the employee does not habitually carry out his work in any one country, by the law of the country in which the place of business through which he was engaged is situated; unless it appears from the circumstances as a whole that the contract is more closely connected with another country, in which case the contract is governed by the law of that country (Article 6 of the Act).

*58.* A special Act implements Directive 96/71/EC concerning the posting of workers for the provision of services, that is the 2007 Act on the Rights and Obligations of Foreign Undertakings that Post Workers Temporarily in Iceland and on their Workers' Terms and Condition of Employment (45/2007). The Act declares that in general Icelandic labour law shall apply to their terms and conditions of employment, irrespective of the foreign legislation covering other aspects of the employment relationship between the worker and the relevant undertaking.

*59.* Iceland is a member of and has ratified the 2007 Lugano Convention on jurisdiction and the recognition and enforcement of judgments in civil and commercial matters, which replaced the 1988 Lugano Convention.

# Part I. The Individual Employment Relation

## Chapter 1. Definition and Concepts

§1. THE DIFFERENT CATEGORIES OF EMPLOYEE

*60.* Employees are divided into different categories by their legal status even though the same basic principles apply to all categories. Unlike in many European countries the Icelandic labour market does not distinguish employees as either white- or blue-collar workers. The main distinction is made between the private and public sector although there is also some special legislation regarding specific categories of employee.

### I. Public Sector Employees

*61.* Public employees have a unique position in the Icelandic labour market. A special legislation focuses the rights and obligations of state employees: the 1996 Government Employees Act (GE Act, 70/1996). Historically, the term 'public employee' has been defined as a person who is appointed to carry out administrative tasks on behalf of the public in state, municipal or public institutions. Under the Act, permanent employees of the state are usually considered to be defined as Government employees. Under the Local Government Act, No. 138/2011, as well as collective agreements, municipal employees enjoy similar rights as state employees. Besides, the 1993 Administrative Act (37/1993) apply to public sector employees, adding to their legal protection on the labour market.

### II. Private Sector Employees

*62.* The concept of private sector employees is considered to include all workers in the labour market, except those who fall under the definition of public employees. No similar Act like the GE Act (or labour code) exists for the private labour market. The rights of private sector employees are stipulated in several Acts, covering different aspects of labour law. Most of these Acts apply also to public employees.

## III. Specific Categories in the Labour Market

63. Legislation regarding the labour market usually stipulates whether its provisions are to cover all private sector employees or only specific categories of worker. It is therefore important to determine whether a worker falls under the definition of a specific category that is subject to special legislation.

### A. Seamen

64. Seamen are considered to be a specific category of workers, and the 1985 Act on Seamen (35/1985) provides special rules regarding their employment. The Act contains provisions on seamen's employment contracts, duration of employment, captains' authority, salaries and other factors regarding employment conditions. The 2007 Act on crews of Icelandic fishing boats, coast guard ships and cruise ships (30/2007) provides additional provisions regarding the safety of ships and their crews, but seamen are exempt from the WEHS Act. Icelandic tax legislation provides seamen with special tax concessions as well as there being special provisions regarding seamen in the 2007 Social Security Act (100/2007).

### B. Foremen

65. On the Icelandic labour market foremen are in fact a mixture of employer and employee, which makes them a specific category in this context. In addition to bearing the same obligations as other employees, foremen have confidentiality obligations to the employer, as they act on his behalf towards employees and have a supervisory function in relation to other employees on behalf of the employer. The obligations of foremen are therefore greater than those of other employees. Stipulations regarding these additional responsibilities and obligations are mainly to be found in the 1980 WEHS Act.

### C. Vocational Trainees

66. The legal status of vocational trainees differs in many ways from that of other employees, since vocational trainees are in fact both students and workers at the same time. The 2008 Upper Secondary School Act (92/2008) provides the general rules concerning vocational trainees. The Act stipulates that the training should contribute to the general education of students, providing them with preparation for certain work and insight into the role of companies and employees in the industry. The programme is also intended to encourage students to maintain their knowledge and add to it with retraining or continuing education. Regulation regarding vocational trainees and training in the workplace contains further provisions regarding vocational trainee contracts and the trainees' status and rights regarding health and safety, supervision and the content of vocational trainee contracts, authorization to evaluate experience for shortening of study time, duties of a company or institution,

conditions which must be fulfilled in order for companies or organizations to be allowed to take students on a vocational trainee contract, probationary period, authorization to provide another place of study if the workplace does not fulfil its obligations and termination of contract.

## IV. Self-Employed Persons

*67.* The legal status of self-employed persons is quite different from that of employees, since contractors are not entitled to the same rights and benefits, including minimum wages, paid vacation and sick days, terms of annulment and unemployment benefits, as employees. Legislation regarding employee rights is in general unwavering and is meant to guarantee certain employee rights and benefits. It is therefore compulsory, and it is not possible to negotiate specific legal employee rights away by contract. These provisions do not in general cover self-employed persons.

*68.* No general statutory definition of the term self-employed exists in Iceland, though the term is defined in the meaning of some Acts, like in the 2006 Act on Unemployment Benefits (54/2006). The term has been developed by courts, but it is not definite since it is evaluated every time whether the person concerned is to be considered an employee or self-employed. The name or form of the contract itself is not the determining factor but the nature/substance of the relationship. The conclusion is based on general assessment of the content of the contract. The definition of employee is implicit in emphasis on subordination, under which an employee obligates himself/herself to work for the employer, under his supervision and responsibility, in return for wages. Many factors contribute to the assessment of contracts to determine the nature of a work relationship. These factors include duration and continuity of the task, separation from general operations, wage-related expenses, facilities, provision of tools and materials, responsibility and risk of the task in question, relationship between the negotiating parties, union affiliation, type of remuneration, sick days, whether the work is carried out personally, independence, vacation pay, tax payments, work supervision and work hours. In practice, judicial rulings play the main role in defining the employee/self-employed status in Iceland.

*69.* No forms of 'employee-like' persons are legally acknowledged in Iceland, and economically dependent workers are not specifically recognized under the labour legislation; therefore no intermediate forms exist between the categories 'employee' and 'self-employed person'.

§2. INDIVIDUAL LABOUR CONTRACTS

*70.* The general rule in Icelandic labour law is that a formal employment contract between an employee and an employer is not a requirement for the establishment of a labour relationship although such relationships are most commonly created through the conclusion of a contract. However, this is not without exception; hence legislation regarding certain categories of employees includes provision making written employment contracts mandatory (*see also* paragraph 27).

## I. Different Categories of Labour Contract

### A. Indefinite Period

71. Employment contracts in Iceland are most commonly concluded for an indefinite period of time and are valid until the contract is terminated by notice from one of the parties. Icelandic legislation does not make any requirement of fixed-term employment contracts in the private sector of the labour market. In the public sector, however, officials shall be appointed for a fixed term of five years. In addition, under the 2008 Act on Public Universities (85/2008) and the 2009 rules for the University of Iceland (569/2009), initial employment in a professor's job and some other academic positions at the University shall normally be temporary and to five years, whether full-time or part-time. In the absence of any stipulations regarding the duration of the contract, it is considered to be valid for an indefinite period. In 1996 the Icelandic Federation of Labour (ASÍ) and the Confederation of Employers (SA) agreed upon including in their collective agreements provisions stipulating that if employees are hired for a longer period than one month and on the average for more than eight hours a week, the employer has the duty to provide a written employment contract or a letter of engagement. An equivalent agreement was made with the state and local government. The agreements were made to implement Council Directive 91/533/EC, on employers' obligations to inform employees of the conditions applicable to the contract or employment relationship, which have general validity as minimal rights in the Icelandic labour market (cf. Ad. B 503/1997).

### B. Definite Period

72. Parties to an employment relationship can agree upon an employment contract that will only be valid for a defined period of time or for the duration of a specific task. A fixed-term contract or a contract by task expires when the period has expired or because the work agreed upon is concluded. The general rules regarding termination of employment contracts do not apply to definite period contracts; hence if they are to be terminated within the definite time period, they have to include a termination clause. When an employment relationship continues unchanged after the expiration of a definite period contract without any formal renewal it is presumed that a contract of indefinite duration has been formed between the parties.

73. No legislation exists in Iceland requiring definite period employment contracts in any field of the private sector of the labour market, but they are commonly used in cases of summer employees and in seasonal occupations and industries. In

the public sector, however, officials are appointed for a certain period of time as well as some academic workers at the University of Iceland (*see* paragraph 71).

74. The Council Directive 1999/70/EC of 28 June 1999 concerning the framework agreement on fixed-term work was incorporated into Icelandic law with the 2003 Act on Fixed Term Employment (139/2003). To prevent abuse arising from the use of successive fixed-term employment contracts or relationships the Act stipulates that a fixed-termed contract may not be extended or be renewed so that it persists continuously for more than two years unless otherwise provided by law. Period of service qualifications relating to particular conditions of employment must also be the same for fixed-term workers as for permanent workers except where different lengths of service qualifications are justified on objective grounds. Furthermore, the Act puts a duty on employers to inform fixed-term workers about vacancies which become available in the undertaking or establishment to ensure that they have the same opportunity to secure permanent positions as other workers.

*C. Trial Period*

75. Employment relationships often begin with a trial period. Unless there are special provisions on trial periods in relevant collective agreements, stipulations on a trial period need to be specified in the individual employment contract. These stipulations have to include the length of the trial period as well as the notice of termination. No general legislation exists in Iceland regarding trial periods in the private sector, but many collective agreements contain provisions on the subject. Typically the trial period is three months but the length of the notice of termination differs. These provisions are generally not compulsory, and parties to an employment relationship are free to agree upon different terms of trial periods if they so choose. If the employment contract is not terminated before the trial period ends, it is presumed that an indefinite period contract has been established (*see also* paragraph 78 in regard to vocational trainees).

76. When it comes to the public sector, the GE Act imposes a trial period but does not stipulate the length of such a period or the notice of termination (Article 41). Directors of government institutions can therefore technically determine the length of trial periods by including provisions in employment contracts or the institution's manual. The length of the trial period is in general stipulated in the individual employment contract or relevant collective agreement. However, even though the Icelandic courts have acknowledged the right to determine the length of trial periods they have also concluded that in the absence of special provisions, the standard trial period of government employees is three months and the mutual notice of termination is one month during that period.

## II. Vocational Trainee Contracts

77. Vocational trainee contracts are defined period contracts in nature, since their purpose is only to last as long as the vocational period in question. Regulation regarding vocational trainees and training in the workplace provides the applicable rules to the contracts which have to be made in writing and in two copies. The agreement provides for the content and arrangements for the vocational training provided.

78. As described above, trial periods are in general not regulated by law in Iceland. However, for vocational trainees it is regulated that probation periods shall be 12 weeks. However, trial time may never exceed one-third of total length of the vocational training, as training will commence at the time the contract is concluded. Each party to the apprenticeship contract can terminate the contract at any time during the probation period without justification.

### A. Form and Content (Written or Unwritten, Mandatory Provisions, Etc.)

79. No formal requirements are necessary to conclude an employment contract. According to judicial precedent, verbal employment contracts are just as valid as written ones. In certain cases a valid employment contract can even be established without any formal relation between the parties. A valid contract of employment can also be based on conduct implying the intention to establish a contract of employment or the commencement of the performance of duties by an employee. Even though a formal employment contract is not a requirement in forming an employment relationship, it is the most common way, and most companies use formal written employment contracts or a letter of engagement in their hiring. The contract or letter of engagement is required to include the following information:

– identities of the parties;
– the place of work and domicile of employer; where there is no fixed or main place of work, the principle that the worker is employed at various places;
– the title, grade, nature or category of the work for which the worker is employed, or a brief specification or description of the work;
– the date of commencement of the contract or employment relationship;
– in the case of a temporary employment, the duration thereof;
– holiday entitlement and holiday allowance;
– length of the notice periods to be observed by the employer and the worker;
– monthly, biweekly or weekly pay, other wage items and the frequency of payment of the remuneration to which the worker is entitled;
– length of the worker's normal working day or week;
– pension fund affiliation;
– the collective agreement governing the worker's terms and conditions of work and the relevant trade union.

*80.* Although in principle a formal employment contract is not required to form an employment relationship, legislation in some instances stipulates requirements for a written employment contract.

*81.* According to the 1985 Seamen Act, shipowners have a duty to provide a written contract. The contract requires a specific form, containing information on the seaman's name, date of birth, address, ranking, wages, other benefits and information regarding period of notice in case of dismissal and termination of employment. The Ministry of the Transport and Local Government has the authority to demand that the contracts be made in a specific form as well as implementing further rules regarding the form of employment contracts in regard to the Act. Shipowners are also required to provide the captain of a ship with a written contract.

*82.* Local governments shall hire a CEO on the basis of the 2011 Local Government Act. The local government body is required to provide the CEO with a written contract, stipulating wages and benefits.

*83.* The GE Act requires the director of a government institution to make written employment contracts with the institution employees (Article 42). The Minister of Finance shall provide further rules regarding employment contracts under the Act.

*84.* The 2002 Foreign Nationals' Right to Work Act (97/2002) contains rules about foreign workers in Iceland. A written employment contract is made a condition for foreign workers receiving a temporary work permit (Article 7).

*85.* The 2005 Act on Temporary-work Agencies (139/2005) requires agencies to provide their employees with a written contract (Article 8).

*86.* Where a written employment contract is required by law or collective agreement, a contract that has not been put down in writing can nonetheless be valid. Under those circumstances the burden of proof lies with the party who maintains the existence of the contract or term of a contract.

*87.* Although parties to an employment contract have some leeway in determining the terms of their agreement, an employment contract may be void in part if the terms of the contract are in violation of the terms of applicable collective agreement, establishing minimum wage requirements and other remunerations or benefits. The same applies to contracts that in any other way reduce the rights guaranteed to workers under legislation. An unlawful contract term can also be set aside, in full or part, or amended according to the 1936 Act on Contracts (7/1936). An unlawful contract term can also lead to the annulment of the contract as a whole.

*B.  Changes in Terms of Employment*

88.  Both parties to an employment contract have a duty to fulfil it on the terms and conditions agreed upon and prescribed by the statutes and collective agreements applicable. If an employer wishes to change the terms of an individual contract of employment to the detriment of the worker, he must do so in accordance with the general notice periods which apply to termination of employment provided for in the contract as well as provisions found in the relevant collective agreement and legislation. An employer can therefore not take any action which has the effect of reducing wages or any of the worker's other significant benefits and rights unless he gives due notice of termination of the contract. The worker is free to consider such a notice of changes as a final notice of termination of his employment contract. Under those circumstances the worker must notify the employer as early as possible. If a worker accepts changes expressly or tacitly the contract will continue after the expiration of the notice. If doubt arises as to whether the worker has accepted the change or not, his silence is regarded as acceptance. The changes come into effect when the notice period has expired if at that point in time the worker has remained in the employment relationship.

*C.  Transfer of Undertakings*

89.  The 2002 Act on Workers' Rights in the Event of Transfers of Undertakings (72/2002), which implements Council Directive 2001/23/EC, on the approximation of the laws of the Member States relating to the safeguarding of employees' rights in the event of transfers of undertakings, businesses or parts of undertakings or businesses, provides for rules on the legal status of employees in the event of transfers of undertakings. The Act stipulates that when an undertaking, or part of one, is transferred to another employer the employees' terms and conditions in accordance with existing employment contracts and collective agreements are transferred to the new employer. A change in ownership or other type of transfer does not constitute grounds for dismissal of employees, unless that is necessary for economic, technical or organizational reasons. However, employees are not obliged to continue their employment under a new employer if the change of ownership implies a change for the worse in their pre-existing terms and conditions of employment.

## III.  Ability to Conclude an Employment Contract

90.  The parties to an employment contract are on the one hand the employer and on the other the employee. The employer can either be a 'physical person' or a 'legal person', but only a physical person can be the employee in the employment relationship.

*A. Competence to Act*

*91.* One of the basic rules in Icelandic law is that a person can only conclude a contract if he or she is legally competent to do so. According to the 1997 Act on Legal Competence (71/1997), a person becomes legally competent when reaching the age of 18. A person not legally competent by reason of minor age who enters into marriage becomes legally competent from the time the marriage takes place. A legally competent person is competent to manage all his or her personal and financial affairs.

*92.* People can be deprived of legal competence either personal, financial or both by judicial decision for reasons of mental illness, mental deficiency or otherwise serious debilitation resulting in incapacity to take care of their affairs in a proper way. Individuals deprived of legal competence are in general not able to conclude contracts of employment without the approval of an appointed guardian. However, a person knowingly concluding an agreement with a person not possessing legal competence without reasonably believing that the guardian's approval has been granted cannot rescind their agreement as long as the person not possessing legal competence performs according to the contract.

*B. Minors*

*93.* Although minors under the age of 18 do not in general have the competence to conclude contracts, Icelandic law does not prohibit them from entering into employment relationships, provided they have the approval of the minor's parents or legal guardian. The WEHS Act (Chapter X) and the 1999 regulation regarding the work of children and adolescents (426/1999) apply to the work of children and adolescents. The legislation does not, however, cover work that takes place temporarily inside a private home or in family businesses that is not considered harmful or dangerous to young people. These rules are based on Directive 94/33/EC, on the Protection of Young People at Work.

## Chapter 2. Rights and Duties of the Parties During Employment

*94.* No general legislation exists regarding the rights and duties of the parties to an employment relationship, although in some cases special legislation is in place regarding certain aspects of the employment relationship as well as certain professions. In the public sector, however, the 1996 GE Act focuses on the rights and duties of state employees. Obviously the essential obligation in any employment relationship is for the employee to work and the employer to pay remuneration. Other rights and duties of the parties can vary based on the type of work in question as well as on both employment contracts and collective agreements.

§1. DUTIES OF THE EMPLOYEE (EXECUTION OF ORDERS, RESPONSIBILITIES, ETC.)

*95.* When entering into an employment relationship, the employee commits himself to perform work for the employer, under his command and responsibility in exchange for remuneration. The employee is therefore under the supervision of the employer and is obliged to comply with the terms of his employment contract.

### I. Duty to Perform Work and Obey Managerial Authority

*96.* The main duty of an employee is to perform the work specified or implied in an employment contract in accordance with the relevant collective agreement. Employment contracts usually contain provisions regarding the type of work or the field of work the employee should perform but rarely specify precise indications or instructions on how the work is to be performed. Specific directions regarding the work are in many cases given verbally by the employer or other managerial authorities. The employee is obliged to comply with orders regarding the work, provided they are within the limitations set by the individual employment contract, collective agreement or relevant legislation. Thus, for the obligation to comply to become effective, orders and directions must be legal and within the framework of employment contracts and collective agreements. Employees are therefore not obliged to comply with orders that involve them breaking the law for example. Furthermore, employees are not obliged to comply with orders that may put themselves or others at risk.

### II. Speed of Work

*97.* In general there are no provisions in employment contracts or collective agreements about the speed of work. Nevertheless, it is a basic rule in Icelandic labour law that work should be performed at a normal speed according to the custom and practice of the trade, taking into consideration an employee's education, work experience, training, etc.

## III. Quality of Work

98.  When it comes to quality of work, the point of view has been taken that the employee has the obligation to perform his work in a proper way. The quality of work should be consistent with the demands of the employer, taking into consideration the custom and practice of the trade as well as the employee's abilities and position.

## IV. Place of Work

99.  The general rule is that employees have the duty to show up and perform their work at a specific place. They are furthermore to arrive and leave the workplace of their own accord, although some collective agreements state that employers are to take employees home from work. This is usually only the case when the place of work in question is far away in a densely populated area or out of reach of public transport. Under the WEHS Act, a place of work is defined as a specified location, either indoors or outdoors, where the employee has to live or spend time on the count of his work. Disputes regarding place of work are rare since it is usually specified in individual employment contracts. Employees are generally engaged to perform their work in the place of work predetermined in employment contracts and are not obliged to perform work in other places. The insistence of an employer on an employee doing so would in most cases be considered to be a breach of the employment contract. In cases where employees are hired to work for an employer with many separate places of operation and without any predetermined place of work, the employee is obliged to do the work at the places decided by the employer.

## V. Duty to Be Loyal

100.  In accordance with general rules on the labour market, employees are duty-bound to be loyal towards their employer. This includes observing the employer's interests in the execution of work and refraining from disloyal conduct even when off-duty. Employees are therefore unauthorized to act against the employer's interests or exploit trade secrets or resources that are of importance to the employer's operations.

101.  The basic principle is that rights and duties in an employment relationship are brought to an end when the relationship is terminated, unless otherwise stipulated in relevant employment contracts. Therefore, if the duty to be loyal is to continue after the conclusion of the employment relationship, it needs to be predetermined in the individual employment contract.

§2. Duties of the Employer

*102.* The main duty of the employer is to pay wages for work done by employees as well as additional social benefits according to national legislation and collective agreements. Furthermore, the employer is duty-bound by law to take certain measures to ensure the welfare and safety of his employees.

## I. Payment of Wages

*103.* As previously stated, the main duty of an employer is payment of wages in accordance with employment contract or collective agreements. The 1930 Act on payment of wages (28/1930) states that wages are to be paid in eligible currency and cannot be paid by debt balance, unless there is a special agreement to that effect. The provision does however not apply to workers whose remuneration is in part received in the form of board and lodging (*see* further in paragraphs 136–139).

## II. Managerial Authority

*104.* As follows from the principle of the worker's duty to obey, previously covered in paragraph 96, an employer asserts a certain managerial authority over his employers. The employment contract itself is based on the presumption that the employer has the right to direct and manage the work done on his behalf within the scope of the contract. However, there are limitations to the authority to direct and manage employees. The employer must comply with any rules stemming from legislation or collective agreements as well as the individual employment contract. Furthermore, when implementing his managerial authority, an employer must act in accordance with what can be considered fair and reasonable.

*105.* Because of the special circumstances that can occur on board ships, the Act on Seamen contains special provisions that authorize captains to force seamen to obey by force if necessary if the ship is in peril or in the case of mutiny for example. All sailors on board are obliged to assist their superior in avoiding damage to the ship or maintaining order. However, if a captain abuses his authority or uses unnecessary severity against his subordinates, he can be subject to penalties or even imprisonment (Article 76 of the Seamen Act).

## III. Safety and Working Environment

*106.* An employer is obliged to ensure full safety and a good working environment and health in the workplace, in accordance with the WEHS Act. An employer has to inform employees of all dangers of accidents and health hazards which may be associated with their work. The employer is also obliged to ensure that employees receive education and training for their jobs to minimize danger associated therewith. Furthermore, the Act stipulates that employers are required to follow provisions of law regarding working environment and health in the workplace, as well as participating and cooperating with safety and labour inspection.

## IV. Obligations Regarding Equality and Sexual Harassment

*107.* Certain obligations are put upon employers regarding gender equality and sexual harassment in the workplace under the Gender Equality Act (10/2008). Employers are to work deliberately to bring women and men on an equal footing in the labour market and specifically take measures to put women and men on an equal footing within their enterprise or institution. Particular emphasis is to be placed on achieving equal representation of women and men in managerial and influential positions. The Act stipulates the duty of equal wages and equal terms of employment for the same jobs or jobs of equal value. Employers are furthermore obliged to take necessary measures to ensure that women and men have equal opportunities regarding retraining, continuing education and vocational training, as well as to attend courses held to enhance vocational skills or to prepare for other assignments or occupations.

*108.* The Gender Equality Act requires employers to take special measures to protect employees, students and clients from gender-based or sexual harassment in the workplace. The Act makes distinction between gender-based harassment, sexual harassment and gender-based violence. Employers shall take special measures to protect employees from gender-based violence, gender-based harassment or sexual harassment in the workplace. Gender-based harassment or sexual harassment constitutes discrimination under the Gender Equality Act, as does all unfavourable treatment of an individual that may be attributed to the fact that the individual has rejected gender-based harassment or sexual harassment, or has submitted to it. Rules concerning actions against sexual harassment in workplaces from 2015 are based on the 1980 WEHS Act. According to the rules, in the making of a health protection plan, according to the Act, the employer shall establish a prevention plan, which includes measures to prevent, e.g., sexual harassment, gender-based harassment and violence at work. The employer must act as soon as possible when he receives a complaint of an indication of sexual harassment, gender-based harassment or violence at work. If a reasoned suspicion is established that this kind of behaviour has taken place, the employer shall take action in accordance with the written plan for safety and health at work in order to stop the behaviour, if it still exists, as well as in order to prevent that the behaviour repeats itself in the workplace.

## V. Tobacco in the Workplace

*109.* Every person's right not to have to inhale air polluted by tobacco smoke from others is to be respected, according to the 2002 Tobacco Control Act (6/2002). The Act further stipulates that smoking is prohibited in the service areas of institutions, business and voluntary organizations, for instance at restaurants and places of entertainment, and where cultural and social activities take place, including sports and leisure activity. The same applies to equivalent outdoor areas, if they are not sufficiently open to ensure adequate ventilation. However, smoking may be permitted in specified guest rooms of hotels and guesthouses. Where smoking is permitted, ventilation shall be ensured meeting the requirements of the health inspectorate, and it shall be ensured that smoke does not pollute the atmosphere of non-smoking areas. The Tobacco Act puts the duty on employers to ensure the employee's right to a smoke-free atmosphere indoors at the workplace.

# Chapter 3. Working Time, Annual Vacations and Holidays

## §1. WORKING TIME

*110.* Working time is regulated through collective bargaining and legislation in Iceland. Hours of daytime work are defined as forty hours per week, divided into five eight-hour working days from Monday to Friday. In general, daytime hours are considered to be between 07:00 and 18:00. The decision as to when during this period workers shall complete the eight-hour workday differs and is decided at each workplace in accordance with the needs of both workers and employers.

*111.* Overtime is defined as those working hours that extend the eight-hour workday and forty-hour workweek. Work performed outside the daytime hours is considered overtime and is remunerated with overtime pay. It is therefore not permitted to pay daytime wages for work done outside the daytime hours, even though the eight-hour workday has not been completed within that time period.

## §2. THE ACT ON WORKING ENVIRONMENT, HEALTH AND SAFETY OF WORKERS

*112.* The WEHS Act follows the requirements put forward in the EU Working Time Directives and lays down minimum safety and health requirements for the organization of working time, including maximum weekly working time, periods of daily and weekly rest, breaks during work hours, aspects of night work, shift work and patterns of work. AOSH is responsible for the enforcement and supervision of the Act. Collective agreements also contain restrictions on working time and the health and safety of workers within the general framework set by the Act.

*113.* The average maximum weekly working time over a four-month reference period stipulated by the Act shall not exceed forty-eight hours per each seven-day period, including overtime. The definition of working time in this context is defined as active working time. Maximum weekly working time may be averaged based on a collective agreement over a reference period not exceeding six months although in exceptional cases this period can be extended to twelve months.

*114.* Daily rest and leisure time should extend over at least eleven consecutive hours for every twenty-four-hour period. If possible, the rest and leisure time should fall within the hours between 23:00 and 06:00. It is unlawful for employers to organize working days longer than thirteen hours. In the case of special circumstances an exception can be made to the rules regarding daily rest and leisure time. In the case of workers specifically being asked to come to work before the eleven-hour daily rest is over or working late to the effect that the eleven-hour rest time will not be completed before they have to start work again, it is allowed to postpone the missing resting time and grant it later as a right to time off work. For every hour of rest reduction 1.5 hours are accumulated. Additionally, exceptions are made in the case of shift work. When workers change shifts and cannot take the mandatory daily rest time between the end of one shift and the start of another, the daily rest may be reduced to eight hours.

*115.* Workers must have at least one day off from work in every seven-day period that should be directly connected to the daily rest. When the coordination of the work requires the postponement of the weekly day off, a special agreement should be made to that effect. Under certain circumstances an employer can, after consulting with his employees, postpone the weekly day off, but this exception should only be used when unavoidable reasons call for it.

*116.* Workers whose regular working hours include more than three hours between 23:00 and 06:00 are considered to be night workers under the Act. Special provisions regarding night workers stipulate that employers are required to take all reasonable steps to ensure that the regular hours of their night workers do not exceed eight hours in every twenty-four hours. Employers are also required to provide night workers with a free health assessment before their assignment as well as thereafter. If a worker suffers from any health problems recognized as being connected to the performance of night work, that worker has the right to be transferred whenever possible to a suitable daytime position. No more than eight hours can be worked in any twenty-four-hour period when night work involves special hazards, heavy physical or mental strain.

*117.* Additionally special provisions apply regarding driving time and rest periods in road transport as well as regarding minors, based on relevant EU Directives.

§3. PART-TIME WORKERS

*118.* According to a general provision in collective agreements, part-time workers are to be treated equally as full-time workers on a pro rata basis. A worker is regarded as a part-time worker if he is paid wholly or partially by reference to the time he works and cannot be identified as a full-time worker when compared to other workers on the same type of contract. Part-time work is addressed in an Act from 2004 (10/2004) which transposed the Part-time Workers Directive 97/81/EC into Icelandic law.

§4. THE ACT ON PART-TIME WORKERS

*119.* The objective of the Act is based on the principle that part-time workers have the right to not be treated less favourably than a comparable full-time worker as regards the terms of his contract of employment. Furthermore, the Act's provisions are meant to improve the quality of part-time work. The Act stipulates that employers are not allowed to discriminate against part-time workers unless it is justifiable on objective grounds. Contractual and statutory rights are to be based on proportional service and a customary working day of the worker concerned.

*120.* The Act specifies that employers are to make arrangements to facilitate more options regarding part-time work while taking workers' interests into consideration. Having worked part-time previously, or currently working part-time, should not prevent a worker from being promoted, whether the new post is full-time or part-time. Additionally, it is unlawful for an employer to terminate a worker for either refusing to go from a part-time position to a full-time position or vice versa.

### §5. Fixed-Term Employment

*121.* A worker who enters into a contract of employment entered directly with an employer where the end of the contract of employment concerned is determined by an objective condition such as arriving at a specific date, completing a specific task or the occurrence of a specific event is in fixed-term employment. The 2003 Act on Fixed Term Employment (139/2003), transposes the Fixed-time Workers Directive 1999/70/EC into Icelandic law.

### §6. The Act on Fixed Term Employment

*122.* The Act on Fixed Term Employment aims to improve the quality of fixed-term work by ensuring the application of the principle of non-discrimination and by establishing a framework to prevent abuse arising from the use of successive fixed-term employment contracts or relationships. The Act stipulates that fixed-term workers are not to be treated in a less favourable manner than comparable permanent workers in respect of employment conditions. Fixed-time workers are not to be discriminated against solely because they have a fixed-term contract, unless different treatment is justified on objective grounds. The Act prohibits the extension or renewal of fixed-term agreements if they last continuously for a period longer than two years, unless otherwise provided for in law. Fixed-term contracts can nonetheless be renewed in the case of managerial personnel, which have been completed for a period of four years or longer, for the same period each time.

### §7. Annual Vacation

*123.* Workers have the right to annual vacation for the purpose of relaxation and recreation. In order to preserve the purpose of the vacation, the worker may not forfeit his time of and take pay or other benefits instead during his vacation. The 1987 Vacation Act (30/1987) provides the minimum rights regarding workers' vacation, but collective agreements provide in many cases further rights depending on different factors.

## §8. THE VACATION ACT

*124.* The Vacation Act provides for a minimum of two working days' vacation for each month in employment during the past vacation allowance year which is from 1 May to April 30. Two weeks or more constitute one month in this respect. The minimum vacation for each year is therefore twenty-four working days. Sundays and other public holidays do not count as vacation days in this respect, nor the first five Saturdays during the vacation. Absence from work due to sickness or accident while the worker is receiving wages, or is on vacation, constitutes working hours for the purpose of calculating the number of vacation days. Collective agreements in many cases contain provisions on broader leave entitlement according to the worker's length of service.

*125.* According to the Act, a worker who is unable to take his vacation at the determined time because of certified illness can demand to be given vacation at another time. Moreover, general collective agreements stipulate that if a worker falls seriously ill during his vacation that he is not able to enjoy it, that time does not count as part of his vacation days, provided he produces a medical certificate.

*126.* Under the Vacation Act, workers are entitled to paid vacation consistent with vacation rights accrued during the past vacation allowance year. The minimum vacation allowance is 10.17% of total wages. If an employment contract is terminated, the employer is required at the end of the employment relationship to pay the worker all his accrued but unpaid vacation allowance.

## §9. VACATION PERIOD

*127.* Summer vacations are to be granted during the period from 2 May to 15 September each year, although provisions can be made in collective agreements for vacation to be taken at other times of the year. This is usually dependent upon particular operational circumstances rendering it necessary. In such cases workers always have the right to take at least fourteen days' vacation time during the summer period. The employer determines, in consultation with workers, when vacation is to be taken, within the summer period. The employer is required to comply with the wishes of his workers as to when vacation is taken, to the extent possible.

## §10. VACATION OUTSIDE THE VACATION PERIOD

*128.* In those cases where workers have to take their vacation outside the standard vacation period, they always have the right to take at least fourteen days' vacation time during the summer period. If workers due to the request of their employer do not take their vacation during the appointed vacation period, they receive a 25% extension of the portion of the vacation taken outside the summer period or equivalent payment.

§11. HOLIDAYS

*129.* In general, after one month of employment with the same employer or in the same occupational sector, workers are not required to perform their duties on special or public holidays, unless they agree to do so. If those days fall within the workweek a normal daytime pay for eight hours will be paid. Work on special holidays is paid with an hourly pay equalling 1.375% of the monthly wages for regular day work, in addition to the eight hours daytime wages. Work performed on public holidays is remunerated with overtime pay, in addition to the eight hours daytime wages.

*130.* Public holidays in Iceland are the following: New Year's Day, Maundy Thursday, Easter Sunday, Easter Monday, First day of Summer, Labour Day (1 May), Ascension Day, White Sunday, White Monday, 17 June (Icelandic National Day), Commerce Day, 24 December from 13:00, 25 December, 26 December, the day before Christmas (Christmas Eve) after 12:00 and 31 December from 13:00.

## Chapter 4. Remuneration and Benefits

*131.* The 1980 WTP Act is the main legal source when it comes to remuneration and benefits of employees. The first article of the Act stipulates the previously mentioned fundamental rule of Icelandic labour law that wages and other working terms agreed between the social partners shall be considered minimum terms, independent of sex, nationality or term of appointment, for all wage earners in the relevant occupation within the area covered by the collective agreement. Contracts made between individual wage earners and employers on worse working terms than those specified in the general collective agreement are void.

*132.* Icelandic legislation does not provide any provisions regarding the amount of wages. Instead collective agreements provide stipulations regarding minimum wages for certain categories of work, either hourly wages and price rates or fixed salaries. Usually minimum wages are the first thing addressed in collective agreements, and the subject of minimum wages is furthermore the main reason for most labour disputes. Employment contracts often include provisions regarding overpay and additional benefits, but in cases where no such stipulations are made between the employer and employee, the provisions of the relevant collective agreement apply.

### §1. THE CONCEPT OF WAGES

*133.* The definition of the term 'wages' is not the same in all cases and is dependent upon the context it is used in. Wages in the sense of collective agreements are considered to be remuneration for work regardless of the form which they are paid. Payment of cost, however, is not considered to be wages. Although the general rule regarding wages is that they are to be paid in an eligible currency, parties to an employment contract are free to negotiate about other forms of payment, provided the remuneration is in no way poorer than the minimum wages agreed upon in collective agreements.

*134.* In addition to negotiation regarding fixed wages, hourly wages, weekly wages, overtime and additional benefits, there has been a tradition in certain fields for social partners to agree upon additional payments associated with performance or achievements. This is most common in the fishing industry.

*135.* It is not uncommon for employment contracts to include provisions regarding various benefits in addition to regular wages. These can include access and use of a car or a phone, free internet access from home and payment of costs relating to transport, meal expenses and clothing, for example. Although payment of cost and various benefits are not considered to fall under the definition of wages they are included in taxable income in accordance with rules published each year by the Internal Revenue Directorate (*Ríkisskattstjóri*).

## I. The Payment of Wages

*136.* The basic rule is that the payment of wages shall be in accordance with provisions in collective agreements and employment contracts. In recent decades the practice has been that employers deposit wages directly into employees' bank accounts although according to judicial precedent an employee has the right to demand to be paid in cash on the basis of the 1930 Act on Payment of Wages (Article 1).

*137.* The due date of wages is in general negotiated in collective agreements. In the private sector, wages are generally paid monthly but in some instances agreements state that wages should be paid weekly or every two weeks. In general, wages are paid (monthly) on the first day after the month ends for which the wages are being paid. However, there is no legislation restricting the parties negotiating for prepaid wages. Traditionally certain categories of workers in the public sector have received prepaid wages although such arrangements have significantly decreased in recent years.

*138.* In the case of errors in wage calculations the general practice has been to seek correction in agreement with both parties. When wages are overpaid, however, there are some restrictions on the reclaim rights of employers. Unless the employee who receives the overpayment ought to have realized the mistake, it is virtually impossible for the employer to claim that the amount of the error be paid back to him. The argument for this practice is first and foremost the interests of the recipients who in good faith have received and used the payment to provide for themselves. Furthermore, it is taken into account that the employer is in a dominant position when it comes to assessing what is the correct payment when he oversees calculations regarding wages. If the wrong calculations on the other hand are based on faulty information from the employee himself, reclaim rights of the employer are in effect. In cases where an error in wage calculations results in underpayment of wages, the employee is entitled to the adjustment of wages as well as penal interest from the time wages were due until the payment date. If wage calculations have been incorrect for a period of time the correction shall include the whole period, provided it is taken into consideration that wage claims expire after four years under Icelandic law.

*139.* In the case of non-payment of wages this is usually presumed to constitute a breach of contract on the behalf of the employer. This is always the case when wages are paid in arrears, and the employee in question has performed work in accordance with the relevant employment contract. In order to collect unpaid wages the employee must use the normal judicial means and the general provisions of claimant law. Even though the employer who fails to pay wages is to pay the entire cost of the collection of the claim, that duty does not come into effect until the final settlement of the claim. Up to that time the employee often has to lay out the costs of the proceedings. Members of trade unions can in these cases seek assistance from their union in collecting such claims and avoid the expenditure.

## II. Wage Deductions

*140.* The Act on Payment of Wages stipulates that employers are not allowed to use a deducted balance to pay wages unless such an arrangement has previously been negotiated upon. Although the stipulation puts great limitations on wage deductions there are certain payments that employers are legally bound to deduct from their employees' wages.

### A. *Taxes*

*141.* Employers are obliged, at a tax collector's demand, to withhold from the wages of employees sufficient to pay dues to entities for which the employees are in self-debt guarantee and are to be collected by tax authorities, according to the 2003 Act on Income Tax (90/2003). If an employer has neglected to withhold dues from wages, the employer is in self-debt guarantee for the payment. Employers are, however, never to withhold more than the amount of 75% of each total wage payment to pay dues. This rule only applies to deductions relating to taxes and does not affect other legitimate deductions.

### B. *Pension Insurance*

*142.* The 1997 Pension Act (129/1997) provides for a mandatory affiliation to a pension fund, for all workers between the ages of 16 and 70. Mandatory pension insurance implies a membership obligation in a pension fund and payment of contributions to a pension fund and, as appropriate, to other parties pursuant to an agreement on supplementary insurance coverage. The membership of an employee's pension fund is generally determined by the relevant collective agreement on which the basic wages are determined or the individual employment contract. Mandatory pension fund membership can in some cases be determinate by special legislation. Where no collective bargaining agreement or special legislation applies to the occupational field concerned, or if the specific terms of employment are not based on a collective bargaining agreement, the worker in question can select a pension fund in accordance with the rules of individual funds. Pension fund membership shall be specified in a written contract of employment. Contributions towards pension rights are determined by special legislation, collective agreements, employment contracts or by other comparable means. Minimum pension contributions shall amount to at least 12%, of which 4% are deducted from the worker's wages and 8% is added by the employer. The contribution base is comprised of all types of wages or compensation for work which are subject to income tax. The contribution does not, however, include benefits paid in kind. Employers are obliged to withhold the amount of the employee's premium part of the pension contribution from the employee's wages and allocate the amount with the employer's contribution to the relevant pension fund.

## C. Union Contributions

*143.* An employer is obliged to deduct from the wages of his employee the employees' contributions payable to the relevant labour union on the basis of the WTP Act. Furthermore, public servants are under the CAPS Act to pay union contributions to the union specified in the relevant collective agreement, regardless of whether or not they are members of a union. In the private sector of the labour market the practice has been the same on the basis of collective agreements.

## D. Child Support Payments

*144.* All parents are liable to provide for their children according to their means, cf. the 2003 Children's Act (76/2003). Non-custodial parents pay child support which is established by either an agreement between the parents or a resolution from the magistrate. An agreement concerning support payments for a child is only valid if confirmed by a magistrate. The State Social Security Institution *(Tryggingastofnun)* pays the child support according to a confirmed agreement to the custodial parent. The Child Support Collection Centre *(Innheimtustofnun sveitarfélaga)* oversees collecting child support payments from non-custodial parents. The centre can, when parents fail to make payments, demand that the parents' employer withhold wages to the required amount, cf. the 1971 Act on the Child Support Collection Centre (54/ 1971). An employer can, however, never withhold more than 50% of an employee's wages for child support payments. If an employer neglects to withhold wages after a requirement to such effect has been received from the Child Support Collection Centre, the employer is responsible for the payment of the amount he has neglected to withhold.

## III. Wage Guarantee Fund

*145.* The 2003 Wage Guarantee Fund Act (88/2003) was enacted with reference to Council Directive 80/987/EEC of 20 October 1980, on the approximation of the laws of the Member States relating to the protection of employees in the event of the insolvency of their employer. The aim of the Act is to guarantee payments to employees and pension funds in respect of their outstanding claims in the event of an employer's insolvency or when the employer's estate at death is settled by an official and his heirs do not accept liability for his obligations. Under special circumstances, the board of the Fund may accept liability for claims without a prior liquidation of the employer's estate, providing that it is clear that the employer has demonstrably ceased operations and that attempts by the claimant to have his estate liquidated have proved unsuccessful, or that the costs of enforcing liquidation would be excessive in the opinion of the board of the Fund.

*146.* The Wage Guarantee Fund guarantees the payment of claims for outstanding wages, compensation for the termination of employment contracts, vacation pay, compensation for accidents at work and pension premiums made against the estate of an employer. The liability period covers claims that have become payable during the eighteen months immediately preceding the date of bankruptcy ruling, or to which entitlement is earned during that period. In case of insolvency of an employer in another EEA Member State employees are entitled to claim unpaid wages if the insolvent employer performed his duties in Iceland. Further, the Wage Guarantee Fund shall exchange information with similar institutions in other EEA Member States. The fund guarantees the following claims:

- claims by employees for wages for their last three months of employment in the service of the employer;
- claims for compensation for loss of wages for up to three months due to the termination of an employment contract, providing that the claimant demonstrates unequivocally, e.g., through registration with a public labour exchange, that he has been on the labour market and has actively sought employment during the termination notice period;
- claims for holiday pay to which entitlement has been earned during the liability period;
- pension funds' claims for pension premiums that have fallen due during the liability period. Liability shall be restricted to the 12% minimum premium and up to 4% of the premium reference based on an agreement on additional insurance cover;
- employees' compensation claims in connection with injuries caused by accidents at work and compensation claims by the relevant party following the death of an employee, providing that these are not covered by the employer's insurance.

*147.* The maximum liability accepted in respect of employees' wage claims is revised each year in regulations issued by the Minister of Welfare following receipt of recommendations from the board of the Wage Guarantee Fund. Part payments of claims made by an employer before the delivery of a liquidation ruling are deducted from the Fund's total liability or the sum falling under guarantee, if it is lower. In the same way, unemployment benefit payments and employment earnings during the notice period are deducted from claims.

*148.* Exemptions from the liability of the Fund are claims by the managing director and directors of the insolvent company which do not qualify for liability. The same applies to the claims of employees who were owners, either alone or together with their spouses or other close associates, of a substantial share of the insolvent company and had a substantial influence on its operations. The Wage Guarantee Fund may furthermore reject claims submitted by the spouses of such individuals, other relatives or persons closely associated with them in other ways if it is demonstrated that their claims are unjustified in terms of the aforementioned connections.

## IV. Equal Wages

*149.* One of the aims of the Gender Equality Act is to work against wage discrimination and other forms of gender-based discrimination in the labour market. Under the scope of the Act wages and terms are defined as all ordinary remuneration for work and further payments of all types, direct and indirect, whether they take the form of perquisites or other forms, paid by the employer to the employee for his or her work. The definition furthermore includes pension rights, holiday rights and sick leave rights and all other terms of employment or entitlements that can be evaluated in monetary terms. On the basis of the Act it is illegal for an employer to apply less favourable employment condition, remuneration or other benefits to an employee than those which applied to employees of the opposite sex for equal work (*see* further in paragraphs 215–217).

## Chapter 5. Incapacity to Work

*150.* As stated in Chapter 3, the main duty of an employee is performing work and not doing so would in general constitute a breach of contract. Under certain circumstances employees can have lawful reasons for not attending work, and in such cases the rule of duty to perform work does not apply.

### §1. ILLNESS AND ACCIDENTS

*151.* The 1979 Act Respecting Labourers' Right to Advance Notice of Termination of Employment and to Wages on Account of Absence through Illness and Accidents (TEIA Act, 19/1979) provides workers with basic rights in case of absence from work due to sickness or accidents occurring in the worker's free time. These rights are further improved upon in collective agreements. These rights are compulsory, and any agreement between an employer and an employee which reduces the employee's rights is invalid.

*152.* In accordance with the above-mentioned Act, a worker who is unable to perform his normal duties at work due to illness or accidents occurring in the employee's free time is entitled to wages from his employer for a certain period of time. The minimum rights during the first year of service with an employer are two days in respect of each month. After one year of employment the employee is entitled to total wages for one month out of every twelve months, after three years with the same employer one month of total wages and one month with day wages out of every twelve months and finally after five years with the same employer one month of total wages and two months with day wages out of every twelve months.

*153.* In cases where employees are excused from work on account of accident at work, on direct route to or from work or due to occupational diseases, they have the right to receive payment of wages for daytime work for up to three additional months. The employer is furthermore bound to pay for all medical expenses stemming from work-related accidents, provided that the cost is not refunded by the worker's health insurance or social security.

*154.* The rights of public employees to payments in case of illness and accidents are governed by collective agreements.

### §2. PREGNANCY AND CHILDBIRTH

**I. Pregnancy**

*155.* In general, the rights of employees who are ill during pregnancy are in no way different from the previously mentioned rights regarding illness. However, there are certain measures taken to guarantee the safety and health in the workplace which are stipulated in the 2000 Act on Maternity/Paternity Leave and Parental

Leave (MPL Act, 95/2000), and the 2000 regulation regarding measures to increase health and safety in the workplace for women who are pregnant, have recently had children or are breastfeeding children (931/2000). Provisions of directive 92/85/EBE, on the introduction of measures to encourage improvements in the safety and health at work of pregnant workers and workers who have recently given birth or are breastfeeding, have been implemented into the two above-mentioned acts of legislation.

*156.* If the safety and health of a pregnant woman, a woman who has recently given birth to a child or a woman who is breastfeeding a child, are considered to be in danger according to a special assessment, her employer shall make the necessary arrangements to ensure the woman's safety by temporarily changing her working conditions, working tasks or working hours (Article 11 of the MPL Act). Changes made are not to affect wages so as to reduce them or abridge other job-related rights. If this is not possible, for valid reasons, the employer is to grant the employee her leave of absence for the length of time necessary to protect her safety and health. When it is necessary to grant a pregnant woman leave, she shall be entitled to payment.

*157.* The above-mentioned regulation regarding measures to increase health and safety in the workplace for women who are pregnant, have recently had children or are breastfeeding children specifies cases where the work of pregnant women is prohibited because of circumstances that could be dangerous or unsafe to their health. The regulation furthermore stipulates that it is prohibited to force a pregnant woman to work at night, if deemed necessary for her safety and health. If changes to the working hours of a pregnant woman cannot be carried out she has the right to a leave of absence provided it is necessary to protect her health.

## II. Maternity/Paternity and Parental Leave

*158.* Parents who are active in the labour market have a right to be granted maternity/paternity leave and parental leave under the MPL Act. The same applies to parents who are self-employed and to parents who are not active in the labour market and parents attending full-time educational programmes as to receiving a maternity/paternity grant. The Act aims to ensure children's access to both their parents and enable both women and men to coordinate family life and work outside the home.

### A. *The Right to Take Maternity/Paternity Leave*

*159.* Each parent has an independent entitlement to maternity/paternity leave for up to three months due to a birth, primary adoption or reception of a child in permanent foster care. In addition, parents have a joint entitlement to an additional three months, which either parent may draw in its entirety or which the parents may divide between them. The individual right of each parent to receive three months maternity/paternity leave is in general not transferable between parents. However, should one of the parents die before the child reaches the age of twenty-four months, the right to maternity/paternity leave which the deceased has not utilized is reverted to the surviving parent. Additionally, a parent who, due to illness, the consequences of an accident or the service of a prison sentence, is unable to care for her/his child during the first twenty-four months may assign the unused entitlement to the other parent, in part or in its entirety. A parent acquires the right to maternity/paternity leave for up to nine months if the other parent has died during pregnancy and the child is born alive. The same applies to single mother who has undergone artificial fertilization or single parent who has an adopted child or taken a child in a permanent foster care.

160. A parent's right to maternity/paternity leave is conditional on the fact that the parent in question has custody of the child or has joint custody with the other parent at the time. A non-custodial parent is entitled to maternity/paternity leave if the consent of the parent exercising custody is obtained, authorizing the non-custodial parent to have access to the child during the period of the leave.

161. Parents have an independent right to maternity/paternity leave, each of up to three months in the event of a stillbirth after twenty-two weeks of pregnancy. In the event of a miscarriage after eighteen weeks of pregnancy, the parents have a joint right to maternity/paternity leave of up to two months from the date of the miscarriage.

B. *The Structure of Maternity/Paternity Leave*

162. The right to maternity/paternity leave is established upon the birth of a child. However, it is permitted to start maternity/paternity leave up to one month prior to the expected birth date, which shall be confirmed by a medical certificate. A mother is required to take maternity leave for at least the first two weeks after the birth of her child. In the case of adoption of a child, or the taking of a child into permanent foster care, the time reference is based on the date when the child enters the home. The right to maternity/paternity leave in connection with the birth of a child expires when the child reaches the age of twenty-four months and in connection with adoption or permanent foster care it expires twenty-four months after the child arrives in the home.

163. A parent has the right to utilize the maternity/paternity leave in a one continuous period or to make arrangements with his or her employer to divide the leave into number of periods, of no less than two weeks at a time, or take the leave concurrently with a reduced work time ratio. Under the Act, employers are duty-bound to make every effort to meet the wishes of their employees regarding the structure of maternity/paternity leave under this provision.

164. The legislation has provisions for exceptions from the regular structure of the maternity/paternity leave in exceptional circumstances (Articles 16 and 17). In

the case of multiple births, parents have a joint right to the extension of maternity/ paternity leave by three months for each child after the first that is born alive or is stillborn after twenty-two weeks of pregnancy. Also, parents who adopt, or take into permanent foster care, more than one child at the same time shall have a joint right to extend maternity/paternity leave by three months in respect of each child after the first. In the event of the child being seriously ill or seriously disabled in a way that demands more intensive parental care than is usual, parents' joint right to maternity/paternity leave may be extended by up to seven months. A mother's maternity leave can also be extended by up to two months due to a serious illness suffered by her in connection with the birth, providing that, during her maternity leave, she has been unable, in the opinion of a medical specialist, of caring for the child due to her illness. Additionally, in cases where it becomes necessary for a pregnant woman, in the opinion of a medical specialist, to cease paid employment for the sake of her health more than a month prior to the expected birth of her child, she shall be entitled to payment during her maternity leave during this period, though not for more than two months.

*C. The Right to Payments from the Maternity/Paternity Leave Fund*

*165.* A parent acquires the right to payments from the Maternity/Paternity Leave Fund after being active on the domestic labour market for six consecutive months prior to the first day of the maternity/paternity leave. A parent's working time in other EEA countries is taken into account if the parent has been employed in Iceland for at least one month during the last six months prior to the first day of the maternity/paternity leave. The work contribution of a self-employed parent shall be based on the payment of the insurance levy on calculated remuneration for the same period. However, in the case of a parent who begins taking maternity/paternity leave before the birth of the child, the date on which the parent begins taking maternity/ paternity leave shall be taken as the base regarding that parent's entitlement.

*166.* The Maternity/Paternity Leave Fund's monthly payment to an employee during maternity/paternity leave shall amount to 80% of her/his average total wages, these being based on a continuous twelve-month period ending six months prior to the birth month or the month the child enters the home for initial adoption or permanent foster care. In 2018 the maximum monthly amount is ISK 370,000. The minimum monthly payment during maternity/paternity leave to a parent in a 25%–49% part-time job shall never be less than ISK 97,786, and the monthly payment to a parent holding a 50%–100% job shall never be less than ISK 135,525. The amounts of maximum and minimum payments are revised in connection with the enactment of the Fiscal Budget every year, to take account of trends in wages, price levels and the economy. However the Minister of Social Affairs and Equality is authorized, with the approval of the Government, to raise the amount in case of significant changes of above-mentioned factors.

### D. *Maternity/Paternity Grants to Parents Who Are Not Active in the Labour Market*

*167.*  Parents who are not active in the labour market, or who are employed in a less than 25% full employment position, each have a separate entitlement to a maternity/paternity grant for up to three months in connection with a birth, primary adoption or reception of the child in permanent foster care which is not assignable. In addition, parents shall have a joint entitlement to a maternity/paternity grant for an additional three months, which either parent may draw in its entirety or the parents may divide between them. The right to a maternity/paternity grant expires when the child reaches the age of twenty-four months. A parent who is outside the labour market, or in less than 25% of full employment each month, shall acquire the right to a maternity/paternity grant for up to nine months if the other parent has died during the gestation period of the child and the child has been born live. The same shall apply in the case of a single mother who has undergone assisted fertilization or a single parent who has adopted a child or taken a child into permanent foster care. A parent must be domiciled in Iceland at the time of the birth of a child, adoption or beginning of permanent foster care, and must have been domiciled in Iceland for the twelve months preceding that date. If the parent was legally domiciled in Iceland for at least some time during the last month preceding the birth of the child, or the date on which the child entered the home in the case of a primary adoption or the taking of the child into permanent foster care, the Directorate of Labour shall, to the extent necessary, take account of her/his periods of residence in another Member State of the EEA, the Nordic Agreement on Social Security, the Convention on the European Free Trade Association (EFTA) or the Agreement between Iceland, on the one hand, and the government of Denmark and the home-rule administration of the Faroe Islands, on the other. The monthly amount of the maternity/paternity grant is ISK 59.137 kr.

### E. *Maternity/Paternity Grant to Parents Attending Full-Time Educational Programmes*

*168.*  In accordance with the MPL Act, parents who were occupied in full-time studies for at least six months during the twelve months immediately preceding the birth, primary adoption or reception of a child in permanent foster care, and met the requirements regarding academic progress during that period, shall each have a separate independent entitlement to a maternity/paternity grant for up to three months in view of the birth, primary adoption or reception of the child in permanent foster care. This entitlement is not assignable. In addition, the parents shall have a joint entitlement to a maternity/paternity grant for an additional three months, which either parent may draw in its entirety or the parents may divide between them. Parents shall submit a certificate from the relevant educational institution stating that she/he has been registered in a full-time programme of studies and met the requirements regarding academic progress during that period. Pursuit of studies, rather than academic achievement, during the academic semester in which the child is born, may be taken into account. Entitlement to maternity/paternity grants expires when the child reaches the age of twenty-four months. Also, a parent who was occupied in full-time studies for at least six months during the twelve months immediately preceding the birth, primary adoption or reception of a child in permanent foster care, and met the requirements regarding academic progress during that period, shall acquire an entitlement to a maternity/paternity grant for up to nine months if the other parent died during the gestation period of the child and the child was born live. The same shall apply in the case of a single mother who has undergone assisted fertilization or a single parent who has adopted a child or taken a child into permanent foster care. The maternity/paternity grant to a parent in a full-time programme of studies shall be ISK 135.525 per month. Normally, the parent shall be domiciled in Iceland at the time of the birth, adoption or beginning of the period of permanent foster care and should have been domiciled in Iceland for the last twelve months preceding that date. Exemptions from the condition regarding domicile may be granted, however, if the parent has transferred her/his domicile temporarily in connection with studies overseas, providing that the parent was domiciled in Iceland continuously for at least five years before the transfer. The same applies when the parent has changed her/his legal domicile on a temporary basis and is pursuing studies at an Icelandic educational institution by distance learning, providing that she/he has been domiciled in Iceland continuously for at least five years prior to the change and meets the other conditions applying to maternity/paternity grants to parents in full-time study programmes. An exception can be made on the requirement regarding satisfactory academic progress, if a mother was not able to pursue studies during the pregnancy for health reasons. In these cases the mother needs to submit a medical certificate from the specialist who attended her during the pregnancy in confirmation of this, together with a certificate from the educational institution stating that she was registered in a full-time programme of studies.

### F. Parental Leave

*169.* A parent is entitled to parental leave for four months to care for his or her child, which is not accompanied by any payment from the Maternity/Paternity Leave Fund according to the legislation. Each parent has an independent right to parental leave, which is not assignable. The right to parental leave is established upon the birth of a child. In the event of adoption, or permanent foster care of a child, account shall be taken of the time when the child enters the home. If a parent has to fetch the child from another country, parental leave may begin at the beginning of the journey. The right to a parental leave expires when the child reaches the age of 8 years. However an entitlement to parental leave that expires without being used, in part or entirely, when the child reaches the age of 8 years, becomes valid once again if the child is later diagnosed as suffering from a serious and chronic illness or severe disability, if this happens before the child attains, in full, the age of 18 years. Rules regarding Maternity/Paternity leave are based on Directive 96/34/EC, on the framework agreement on parental leave.

### III.  Attending Sick Children and Other Compelling Family Reasons

*170.*  General collective agreements provide parents who have worked for six months for the same employer two workdays for each month to attend to their sick children under the age of 13 years, provided that sufficient attendance cannot be arranged in another way. After six months of service with the same employer, parents are likewise permitted to devote a total of twelve days in each twelve-month period to attend to their children under the age of 13 years. During this time the parent has the right to full wages for daytime work, including shift premiums when applicable. Additionally, in cases where an employee's child suffers grave and lasting illness, he can apply for additional payments from his Trade Union Sickness Fund. The same applies if the employee's spouse falls seriously ill or has a serious accident.

*171.*  Employees are furthermore entitled to an unpaid leave from work due to unforeseen and grave reasons (force majeure) or when it concerns very serious illness or accident in their family that requires their immediate presence.

# Chapter 6. Job Security

## §1. GENERAL PRINCIPLES

*172.* As a fundamental rule, both parties to an employment contract are equally authorized to terminate an employment contract without stating a reason. In general, most workers are hired for an indefinite period, in which instance the employment contract is terminated with a notice period as stated in law or the relevant collective agreement. The right to employment termination notice is mutual and such employment cancellations should be in made in writing. It should be noted though that the freedom of the employer to terminate the employment contract is in certain cases restricted by law and/or collective agreements.

*173.* Lifetime employment is not customary in Iceland with the exception of judges which are appointed for life and cannot be discharged from office except by a judicial decision, nor may they be transferred to another office against their will, except in the event of reorganization of the judiciary. However, a judge who has reached the age of 65 may be released from office, but judges of the Supreme Court do not lose any of their wages (Article 61 of the Constitution).

*174.* Fixed-term contracts as well as contracts by task expire when the period has expired or when the work agreed upon is concluded. The general rules regarding termination of employment contracts do not therefore apply to these contracts. If a definite time period contract is to be terminated the prerequisite is made that the contract include a termination clause that stipulates the notice and procedure of termination.

## §2. PROCEDURE OF TERMINATION

*175.* Termination of an employment contract is binding from the time the notice of termination reaches the recipient. Notice of termination is to be in writing and in the same language as the relevant employment contract. However, even though certain statutes and collective agreements require a written notice of termination, a verbal one can be valid but the burden of proof is in many cases more difficult and falls solely on the terminating party. The notice of termination must furthermore be clear and unequivocal.

*176.* After a year of employment, the TEIA Act stipulates that a notice of termination should be based on the turn of the month or week if applicable. If the formal notice of dismissal is not received by the employee at the latest on the last working day of the month, the notice period is automatically pushed back to the turn of the next month. Most collective agreements refer to the above-mentioned provisions, but the rights of employees during the first year of employment can differ.

*177.* Under collective agreements, employees have since 2008 been entitled to an interview regarding the end of employment and the reasons for termination of employment. A request for such an interview shall be given within four days from the notice of termination of employment coming to the employee's knowledge. An employee can request the reasons for termination of employment to be stated in writing. Should the employer fail to fulfil that request the employee is entitled to another interview with the employer in the presence of his or her union representative or other representative of the union, if the employee so requests.

178. In cases of termination, the employment relationship between the parties remains intact and the rights and duties of the parties are unchanged until the end of the notice period. Nevertheless, the parties can come to an agreement to end their relationship before the notice period expires. If an employee is deprived of his right to a lawful notice of termination, he can claim damages equal to the financial loss during the notice period. In the same way, an employer has the right under certain circumstances to claim damages, in cases where an employee leaves without giving the required notice.

§3.  TERMS OF NOTICE IN THE EVENT OF DISMISSAL

179. The TEIA Act establishes statutory minimum rights regarding notice periods. According to the Act the notice period is mutual; hence, the employee who is entitled to the following notice periods is also to give the same notice of termination of employment:

– after one-year continuous employment with the same employer: one month's notice;
– continuous employment for three years with the same employer: two months' notice;
– five years of continuous engagement with the same employer: three months' notice.

180. Collective agreements generally contain further provisions regarding notice periods, applicable during the first year of employment which are in most cases better than the statutory minimum. Furthermore general collective agreements include an increased notice period based on seniority and age of the employee. After at least ten years of consecutive work employment for the same employer, the notice period based on the employees' age is as follows:

– 55 years of age: four months' notice;
– 60 years of age: five months' notice;
– 63 years of age: six months' notice.

181. The employee on the other hand can resign with a three-month notice period. The statutory minimum rights put forward in legislation and collective agreements are compulsory, but parties to an employment relationship can always negotiate better terms in the individual employment contract.

§4. Partial Termination of Contract

*182.* When a company goes through restructuring or a significant decrease in business there may be a need to change the terms of employment contracts, which may include shorter working hours and/or wage decreases. If an agreement regarding such changes in employment cannot be reached with the employees, this often results in termination of employment, either altogether or only partially.

*183.* It is possible to partly terminate an employment contract, but it must be specified exactly which elements of the contract are being terminated. A notice of termination in part constitutes an offer to an employee to continue the employment relationship but under a new employment contract which the employee can either accept or refuse. Either way, the same rules regarding notice periods apply whether the contract is terminated partly or the employee refuses the offer and the contract is terminated altogether. The same rules regarding the procedure of termination of contract apply when the termination is partial. In case of partial termination of an employment contract the employee may be entitled to unemployment benefits under temporary provisions of the Unemployment Act, specifically aimed to avoid redundancies due to the economic recession.

§5. Immediate Dismissal

*184.* As previously stated, generally both parties to an employment relationship can terminate the employment contract without stating a reason. However, immediate dismissals are only considered legitimate in cases of serious misconduct, like severe violations against the provisions of employments contract or the main duties of the employment relationship. Although there are no exhaustive rules regarding the severity of the misconduct needed to justify termination without notice, general principles of contract and labour law apply as well as the assessment put forward through judicial precedent.

*185.* Parties to a contract are obliged to respect and follow its provisions. The main employment contract obligations are the obligations of the employer to pay wages and the employee to perform work. If these obligations are violated, for example wages not paid for some time or the employee refuses to perform the work he is hired to do, this would constitute a significant violation of the employment contract. Under these circumstances an employee may be permitted to terminate the contract without notice and likewise the employer can dismiss the employee without notice. Termination without notice on the basis of violation of employment contract requires the violation to be significant and/or repeated. Violations carried out deliberately or by gross negligence are therefore usually considered to provide a justification for immediate dismissal although each instance always has to be independently evaluated.

*186.* In most cases, a warning administered by the employer in a verifiable manner is a prerequisite for termination. With the warning, the employee is made aware of his violation and given an opportunity to improve. The termination must be made based on a second breach of contract of the same nature as the previous one resulting in a warning. A prior warning must also state specifically that if the behaviour is continued by the employee, it can result in a termination of contract without notice. A warning should be administered as soon as possible after the employer becomes aware of the violation. The warning must be verifiable, either by witnesses or by being in written form, but otherwise there are no formal requirements for such warnings. Generally, the duty of administering a warning before terminating a contract also applies to employees, but there are fewer requirements regarding the formality of the warning.

*187.* Misconduct or violations can be so serious that they justify termination without a prior warning. Severe violations such as theft, embezzlement, forgery or violence at the workplace usually justify termination without warning. Violations of the Penal Code (19/1940) in nearly all cases constitute a justification for termination without notice. Nevertheless, a suspicion of the previously mentioned violations does not validate a termination and can make the employer subject to liability.

*188.* Where employment contracts are terminated without notice the party who terminates can become liable to the other party if there were no justifiable reasons for termination. The employee usually has the right to wages in accordance with the notice period he is entitled to, and in some cases he might also be entitled to damages. When an employee terminates the contract without notice he can become liable if the termination has caused damage of some sort to the employer. The policy of employee liability is, however, viewed with caution and in accordance with the 1993 Act on Torts (50/1993, Article 23) where it is stated that it is only possible to claim compensation from an employee if it can be perceived as fair in view of the circumstances.

§6. COLLECTIVE DISMISSALS

*189.* The 2000 Collective Redundancies Act (63/2000) is based on Council Directive 98/59/EC, on the approximation of the laws of the Member States relating to collective redundancies. Collective dismissals are to be announced by employers when they affect employees for reasons that they are in no way responsible for. The definition of collective dismissals put forward in the Act in terms of the minimum number of employees who are to be dismissed is as follows:

– at least ten workers in enterprises usually employing more than 20 and less than 100 persons;
– at least 10% of all workers in enterprises usually employing more than 100 and less than 300 persons;
– at least 30 workers in enterprises usually employing at least 300 workers.

*190.* An employer contemplating a collective dismissal has the duty to consult with employees or their representatives and provide them with the opportunity of making suggestions on how to avoid the dismissals or to limit the number of dismissals and to alleviate their consequences. The employer is furthermore obliged to provide employees or their representative body with all relevant information concerning the dismissals. Information regarding following issues are to be in writing:

– the reasons for the collective dismissal;
– the number of workers to be dismissed;
– the number of persons usually employed;
– the time period within which the notification of the dismissals is to be given.

*191.* The employer is also required to notify the regional employment office in the relevant area of the proposed collective dismissals.

§7. TRANSFER OF UNDERTAKINGS

*192.* The 2002 Act on Rights of Employees at Transfer of undertakings (72/2002) is based on Council Directive 2001/23/EC. The Act applies to any transfer of an undertaking, business or part of an undertaking or a business within EEA, in a Member State of the Convention establishing EFTA or in the Faeroe Islands. The Act does not, however, apply to seagoing vessels or administrative reorganization of public administrative authorities, or the transfer of administrative functions between public administrative authorities.

*193.* In cases of transfers of undertakings, in part or in whole, the terms and conditions from existing contracts of employment and collective agreements are transferred to the new employer, including the transferor's breach of his duties prior to the transfer. During the transfer proceedings, the transferor is required to inform employees or their representatives in good time, before the transfer is carried out, about the following:

– the date or proposed date of the transfer;
– the reasons for the transfer;
– the legal, economic and social implications of the transfer for the employees;
– any measures envisaged in relation to the employees.

*194.* The transferee must give such information in good time and in any event before his employees are directly affected by the transfer as regards their conditions of work and employment. Where the transferor or transferees envisage measures in relation to their employees, they are required to consult employees or employee representatives on such measures and try to reach an agreement. Transfers of undertakings or other changes in ownership do not constitute grounds for dismissal of employees, unless they are necessary for economic, technical or organizational reasons. Employees are, however, not obliged to continue their employment under a new employer if the change of ownership implies a change for the worse in their pre-existing terms and conditions of employment. Finally, if either the transferor or transferee violates the provisions of the Act, by intention or negligence, that person is liable for damages according to general rules of law.

### §8. Public Employees

*195.* For termination of employment, special rules apply when it comes to public employees. In the public sector the GE Act is the main legal source for state employees, but for local government employees the relevant collective agreements apply. Furthermore, the rules of the 1993 Administrative Procedure Act and the general rules of administrative law apply, for example the rule that every administrative decision shall be based on objective grounds. For state employees, a distinction is made between civil servants on the one hand and all other state employees (general employees) on the other. Civil servants, defined as officials in the highest governmental positions, are usually appointed for a five-year term. Other employees of the state are generally hired for an indefinite period with a mutual notice period. For these groups different procedural rules of dismissal apply and within each group the applicable rules may vary depending on which grounds the dismissal (or removal from office) are based. In all cases public employees can demand written justification after the termination of the employment contract, where the reasons for the termination must be described.

### §9. Special Protection of Certain Categories of Employee

*196.* Certain categories of employee in the labour market are granted special protection from termination in the light of their position. Nevertheless, the protection is not without limitations and does not protect employees from termination on the basis of objective and lawful grounds.

## I. Trade Union Representatives

*197.* Trade union representatives hold a special position in the Icelandic labour market, and the TUI Act provides them with special protection when it comes to dismissals.

*198.* Employers and their representatives are not permitted to terminate the employment of trade union representatives on account of their service as such or to allow them in any way suffer for the fact that a trade union has charged them with discharging shop steward duties for the union. If an employer needs to reduce the number of workers, a shop steward shall, other things being equal, have priority in retaining his or her job. If a shop steward loses his authority on the transfer of an undertaking he shall, however, enjoy protection as such under legislation and agreements, according to the Act on Rights of Employees at Transfer of Undertakings.

The protection of trade union representatives is limited to the number of union representatives that the union is entitled to nominate under law and collective agreements.

*199.* The protection granted to trade union representatives is not without limitations. It has been considered legitimate to terminate the employment contract of a shop steward due to age, in the same way as for other employees, provided the age limit set by the employer is legitimate and non-discriminatory. Furthermore, the shop steward protection does not cover termination on the basis of misconduct or violation of employment contract. In cases of unjustified dismissals of trade union representatives the employer is liable, but will not be subject to reinstatement.

*200.* Safety representatives and the representatives of the employees on the safety committee, under the WEHS Act, are similarly guaranteed the protection described above like union representatives.

## II. Pregnant Women and Those Taking Maternity/Paternity or Parental Leave

*201.* Employers are under the MPL Act prohibited from terminating a worker due to the fact that he has given notice of intended maternity/paternity leave or parental leave. The same applies during maternity/paternity leave or parental leave, without reasonable cause, and in such a case, the dismissal must be accompanied by written arguments. The same rule applies to pregnant women and women who have recently given birth. The employment relations between an employee and her/his employer shall remain unchanged during maternity/paternity leave and parental leave, and the employee is entitled to return to her/his job upon the completion of maternity/paternity leave or parental leave. Where this is not possible, the employee is entitled to a comparable position with the employer according to a contract of employment.

## III. Workers Having Family Responsibilities

*202.* The 2000 Act on Prohibition on Termination of Employment due to Family Responsibilities (27/2000) is based on the ILO's Workers with Family Responsibilities Convention, No. 156 (1981). The principal rule is that an employment contract may not be terminated solely because of a worker's family responsibilities. The term 'family responsibilities' refers to the employee's responsibilities towards his or her children, spouse or close relatives who live in the employee's home and clearly needs his or her care or custody, for example as a result of illness or disability. Three principal conditions must be met to demonstrate the existence of family responsibilities:

– the responsibilities must be towards the worker's own children, spouse or close relatives;

– the persons concerned must live in the workers own home;
– the person or persons involved must need the care or guardianship of the worker himself in connection with, e.g., illness, disability or comparable circumstances.

All three preceding conditions must be met in order for the worker to be regarded as bearing family responsibility under the Act.

## IV. Gender

*203.* The Gender Equality Act includes prohibition of dismissal on the basis of gender. Furthermore, employers may not dismiss employers for demanding redress on the basis of the Act. The Act also prohibits any discrimination regarding termination of contract and forbids anyone to waive the rights set forth in that section of the law.

## V. Part-Time Workers

*204.* It is not alone a valid reason to terminate employment contract because an employee refuses to move from full-time to part-time or vice versa, cf. the 2004 Part Time Work Act. If termination complies with law, collective agreements or practice and is due to other reasons than described above, such as the operational needs of the organization, this is not contrary to the Act.

## VI. Transfer of Undertakings

*205.* A transfer of an undertaking does not in itself constitute valid grounds for dismissal, cf. the 2002 Transfers of Undertakings Act. This does not, however, prevent dismissals for economic, technical or organizational reasons entailing changes in the workforce.

# Chapter 7. Protection of Certain Categories of Worker and Protection Against Discrimination in Employment

*206.* The human rights section of the Icelandic Constitution stipulates that everyone shall be equal before the law and enjoy human rights irrespective of sex, religion, opinion, national origin, race, colour, property, birth or other status (Article 65). The broad scope of the article has been presumed to cover all aspects of society including the labour market. No general legislation regarding discrimination in the labour market exists in Iceland, but the 2008 Gender Equality Act as well as the 1992 Disability Act (59/1992) includes provisions regarding discrimination and access to the labour market. Icelandic legislation does not include provisions against discrimination in the private labour market with respect to age, sexual orientation or religion. However, the public sector falls under the scope of the 1993 Administrative Procedures Act. The Act stipulates that when deciding cases a public authority shall make every effort to ensure that, legally, it is consistent and observes the rule of equal treatment. Furthermore, the parties to a case may not be discriminated against on the grounds of their ethnic origin, sex, colour, nationality, religion, political conviction, family or other comparable considerations (Article 11). It should be noted, though, that the implementation of the EEA Agreement prevents discrimination based on nationality. In addition, Iceland has ratified several international and European human rights conventions which include equal rights protection on the labour market. The 2018 Act on Equal Treatment of workers (86/2018) applies, cf. Article 1, to equal treatment of individuals in the labour market regardless of race, ethnic origin, religion, belief, disability, impaired working capacity, age, sexual orientation, gender identity or sexual expression, such as access to employment, self-employment or occupation, including with recruitment and progress at work; access to educational and vocational counselling, vocational education and training; decisions relating to salary, other terms of employment and terminations of employment and participation in employer's organizations or labour unions, including the benefits they provide to members. The purpose of the Act is to combat discrimination and establish and maintain equal treatment of individuals in the labour market. Employers may, with few exceptions, not discriminate between applicants for employment for any of the factors referred to in Article 1 of the Act. The same applies to promotion, status change, retraining, lifelong learning, vocational training, study permits, termination, working conditions and other employee benefits. Under the Act, discrimination to any of the factors referred to in Article 1 in the advertisement on a vacant job is, with few exceptions, prohibited as well as the publication of such advertisements. An employer may not discriminate against his employees for any of the factors referred to in Article 1 in relation to wages and other benefits, when they have the same job or job of equal value. Different treatments based on any of the factors referred to in Article 1 are not considered to be in violation of the Act if it is based on the nature of the activity in question or the context in which the activity is conducted, provided that requirements for such job-related features have legitimate purpose and do not go beyond what is necessary. Also, specific temporary measures designed to improve the position of individuals in the labour market in areas where there is a disadvantage for any of the factors referred to in Article 1, in order to promote equal treatment in the labour market, are not in violation of the Act. In addition, different treatment based on age is considered not to be in violation of the Act, if it is substantiated by a legitimate reason, including a legitimate purpose, employment policies or other labour market objectives, provided such actions do not go beyond what is considered necessary to achieve the objective pursued. Employers may not terminate employment of workers because they have complained of or opposed discrimination on account of any of the factors referred to in Article 1 or required correction based on the Act. Violations of the Act may be subject to liability or fines, unless heavier punishment is in accordance with other laws.

## §1. PEOPLE WITH DISABILITIES

*207.* The objective of the 1992 Disability Act is to ensure for people with disabilities' equality and living conditions comparable with those of other citizens and to provide them with conditions that enable them to lead a normal life. People with disabilities are to be given priority regarding work for the state and municipalities if their qualifications for a given post are greater or equal to those of other applicants. If a Regional Board is of the opinion that the rights of a person with disability have been disregarded in the granting of an employment position, the Board can request a written explanation for the decision regarding the appointment from the appointing authority. Additionally, each operational region shall offer people with disabilities with sheltered work on the labour market. Special sheltered workshops for people with disabilities may also be operated. The purpose of such sheltered workshops is twofold: on the one hand they provide remunerated training for people with disabilities to enable them to work on the general labour market, and on the other, they provide remunerated regular jobs for people with disabilities.

*208.* In accordance to the Act each operational region must have a selective placement service, with the purpose of obtaining suitable work for people with disabilities. In connection with this placement service, occupational counselling shall be provided. Where municipalities operate a special employment bureau, this bureau shall be entrusted with the operation of a selective placement service for people with disabilities under a special agreement. People with disabilities shall furthermore be given assistance in holding jobs on the general labour market when necessary, through special personal support at the workplace as well as through information and instruction for other workers.

*209.* Even though the Disability Act stipulates that people with disabilities should be given priority regarding work in the public sector the law does not include similar provisions regarding the private sector of the labour market. The 2018 Act on Equal Treatment of workers (86/2018) applies however, cf. Article 1, e.g., to equal treatment of disabled individuals and prohibits discrimination on the basis of disability on the labour market (*see* paragraph 208). In addition, the Act stipulates (Article 10) that the employer shall take appropriate measures, if necessary in special cases, to enable a disabled person or person with reduced working capacity to gain access to and take part in employment, to get a job progress or receive train-ing, provided that such measures are not too burdensome for employer.

## §2. MINORS

*210.* The work of children and youths is subject to the rules of the WEHS Act and the Regulation concerning Work of Children and Youths (426/1999). These are based on Directive 94/33/EC, on the Protection of Young People at work. Limita-tions are set with regard to the type of work, working environment and working time. The Regulation classifies young workers into three groups:

(1) youth – an individual under the age of 18;
(2) child – an individual under the age of 15 or who is still in compulsory school-ing;
(3) adolescent – an individual who has reached the age of 15 but is younger than 18 and is no longer in compulsory school.

*211.* The aim of the regulation is to ensure the safety and mental and physical health of young people in the workforce. The work undertaken by young people must not have disturbing effects on their education or development. Furthermore young workers have a right to particular assistance and care by the employer. Employers are required to inform other workers, who work with young people, as well as those in charge of safety measures, of the demands that are made on the work of young people and ensure that they are abided by and that they are followed in the execution, organization and supervision of the work of young people.

## I. Prohibited Work

*212.* The regulation imposes several provisions which prohibit certain kinds of work for young people in the interests of protecting their health and development. These prohibitions include work with dangerous tools and equipment and toxic sub-stances. Children under the age of 15 or still in compulsory school may only engage in work that falls under the definition of light work. Children may work neither with or in the vicinity of machinery or dangerous substances and nor should they lift heavy weights.

## II. Working Hours

*213.* The working time of adolescents must not exceed eight hours per day and forty hours per week. In special instances, exceptions can be made in case of press-ing need due to the nature of the operation; for example, if valuables in agriculture or fish processing need to be saved, the work time of adolescents may exceed eight hours per day and forty hours per week, provided that the provisions of daily rest and time off are honoured. Working hours may not exceed more than sixty hours per week and forty-eight hours per week average over a four-month period. The regulation also provides for a minimum daily rest, which shall not be less than twelve hours of consecutive rest. Furthermore, adolescents must receive at least two days off during every seven-day period.

*214.* Children aged 13–15 can take part in work in relation to cultural and arts events as well as sporting events and advertising. The working time of children of age 13–15 is further limited, and employers are to take their age and maturity into special consideration.

# Chapter 8. Gender Equality

*215.* In Iceland, comprehensive gender equality legislation has been in place for years and has been amended on a regular basis. The 2008 Gender Equality Act is wide-ranging legislation including most spheres of society, and section III of the Act contains provisions regarding the labour market.

*216.* The Act prohibits all forms of discrimination, direct or indirect, on the grounds of gender although affirmative action is not regarded as being contrary to the Act. The same applies if there are valid reasons to support employing an individual of a particular gender in view of objective factors relating to the job. The Act stipulates that women and men shall enjoy equal rights in all respects, and women and men working for the same employer are to paid equal wages and enjoy equal terms of employment for the same jobs or jobs of equal value. Equal wages in this respect means that wages are to be determined in the same way for women and men, and as a measure to ensure this, employees are at all times permitted to disclose their wage terms if they choose to do so. If it happens that a woman and a man working for the same employer receive different wages for the same work, or for work of equal value, the employer must demonstrate, if there is a difference in their wages, that the difference is explained on the grounds other than their gender.

*217.* In addition to wages, employers may not discriminate between women and men in other terms of employment on the grounds of their gender. Employers are furthermore prohibited from discriminating between applicants for jobs on grounds of their gender. The same applies regarding promotion, changes of position, retraining, continuing education, vocational training, study leave, notice of termination, the working environment and employees' working conditions. It is also prohibited to allow maternity/paternity or parental leave, or other circumstances relating to pregnancy and childbirth, to have a negative effect on decisions on an employee's working conditions or development. If likelihood is adduced that individuals have been discriminated against on the grounds of their gender, the Act puts the duty upon the employer to demonstrate that decisions regarding the employer are based on other grounds than the individual's gender.

*218.* Additionally, employers are to take all necessary measures to enable women and men to reconcile their professional obligations and family responsibilities. Among other things, such measures shall be aimed at increasing flexibility in the organization of work and working hours in such a way as to take account of both the worker's family circumstances and the needs of the labour market, including facilitating the return of employees to work following maternity/paternity or parental leave or leave from work due to pressing and unavoidable family circumstances. Finally, employers may not dismiss employers for demanding redress on the basis of the Equality Act and are to ensure that employees are not subjected to injustice in their work, with regard to job security, terms of employment or performance assessment, on the grounds of having submitted a complaint or provided information regarding gender-based or sexual harassment or sexual discrimination.

*219.* Violations against the Act, either deliberate or through negligence, lead to liability to pay compensation according to the ordinary rules. The party in question may also be sentenced to pay the party affected by the violation compensation for non-financial loss, if appropriate, in addition to compensation for financial loss. Furthermore, violations of the Act can be punishable by fines to the State Treasury unless heavier penalties are prescribed in other statutes.

§1. Measures to Promote Gender Equality in the Labour Market

*220.* In addition to provisions regarding discrimination, the Gender Equality Act implements certain measures to promote gender equality in the labour market. In the effort to put women and men on an equal footing in the labour market, enterprises and institutions with more than twenty-five employees, on average over the year, are to set themselves a gender equality programme or insert mainstream gender equality perspectives into their personnel policy which are at three-year intervals. Upon request, enterprises and institutions shall provide copies of their gender equality plan, or personnel policy if they do not have a gender equality programme, together with their action plan to the Centre for Gender Equality. Where an enterprise or institution with more than twenty-five employees does not set itself a gender equality programme or mainstreamed gender equality perspectives into its personnel policy or fails to provide copies of such upon the request of the Centre for Gender Equality, the Centre may determine that the enterprise or institution in question is to pay per diem fines until it complies with the instructions. Decisions to impose per diem fines may be enforced by attachment. Appeals lodged with the Minister of Welfare or litigation before the ordinary courts do, however, defer enforcement action. In 2017 the system of Gender Equality Certification (Jafnlaunavottun) was established by amendment to the Gender Equality Act. A company or institution with an average of twenty-five or more employees on an annual basis shall acquire certification, following the certification body's audit of the company's or institution's equal pay system in which it is confirmed that the equal pay system and the implementation thereof meet the requirements of the ÍST 85 standard. Once certification has been finalized, the certification body shall send a copy of the certification certificate to the Centre for Gender Equality, together with a report on the outcome of the audit. Certification shall be renewed every three years. The certification body shall also inform the Centre for Gender Equality if the audit does not result in certification and state the reasons for this by submitting a report on the outcome of the audit. When the Centre for Gender Equality has received a certification certificate along with the certification body's report on the outcome of the audit, the Centre shall award an equal pay symbol to the company or institution based on the certification, or equal pay recognition to the company or institution based on the confirmation and the equal pay recognition shall remain valid for the duration of validity of the confirmation. The Centre for Gender Equality shall maintain a register of companies and institutions that have acquired certification. The Act also stipulates that the social partners shall monitor to ensure that companies and institutions which employ an average of twenty-five or more employees on an annual basis acquire with certification or confirmation in accordance, and that these are renewed. Companies and institutions shall provide the organizations of the social partners with the information and documents that the organizations of the social partners consider necessary for them to be able to conduct their monitoring. If a company or institution has not obtained certification or renewal has not been obtained, or if it fails to provide the necessary information or documentation, the organizations of the social partners may report this to the Centre for Gender Equality. The Centre may instruct the relevant company or institution to take adequate corrective action within a reasonable time or face a penalty through the imposition of per diem fines.

*221.* When appointments are made to national and local government committees, councils and boards, measures shall be taken to ensure equal representation of both genders, and not less than 40% of one gender when there are more than three representatives in a body. This also applies to the boards of publicly owned limited companies and enterprises in which the state or a municipality is the majority owner. When nominations are made to national and local government committees, councils and boards, both a man and a woman shall be nominated, unless this is impossible due to objective circumstances.

*222.* In March 2010 the Icelandic Parliament amended the 1995 Act respecting Public Limited Companies (2/1995), and the 1994 Act respecting Private Limited Companies (138/1994), implementing gender quotas on company boards. The amendment entails that in companies with more than fifty employees, on average over the year, both genders should be represented on the board of directors, and when the board is composed of more than three members the proportion of each gender shall not be lower than 40%. The same applies to the gender ratio among alternates. When reporting on the assembly of board of directors to the Register of Limited Companies (*Hlutafélagaskrá*), there shall be an analysis of gender ratios. Furthermore, companies with more than twenty-five employees on average shall also turn in analysis of gender ratio statistics relating to both employees and management. Additionally, all companies who fall under the scope of the Act shall take gender ratio perspectives into consideration in the recruitment of CEOs and report statistics thereof to the Register of Limited Companies.

## Chapter 9. Covenants of Non-competition

*223.* Clauses restricting competition are most commonly used in employment relationships, and it is quite common for employment contracts to include such a clause. These restrictions particularly concern the period after the employment relationship ends, i.e., they restrict the employee being employed in a competing enterprise or setting up as self-employed within the same trade. Covenants of non-competition restricting one party's right to compete with another are in general presumed to be valid.

*224.* Nevertheless, the 1936 Act on Contracts, Agency and Void Legal Instruments (7/1936) puts some limitations on the parties' right to negotiate such covenants. If for the purpose of preventing competition, a person has obtained a commitment from another person not to engage in a commercial undertaking or other business, or not take up employment at such an undertaking, the promise is not binding on the person if it must be assumed, in light of all the circumstances, that the commitment goes beyond what is necessary to avoid competition, or if it unreasonably restricts the freedom of employment of the person who undertook the obligation. Furthermore the Act stipulates that if an employee of a commercial undertaking or other enterprise has agreed upon a contract including a clause of non-competition with the person operating the undertaking, and if the commitment is intended to remain in effect after the person's employment at the undertaking is at an end, the commitment shall not be binding if the person's employment is terminated or if he or she is dismissed without having given adequate cause, or if the person lawfully relinquishes the position on the grounds that the person operating the undertaking has failed to meet his obligations.

*225.* Even in the absence of a contract on the matter, it is presumed that an employee has the duty to act in a manner that in no way threatens his or her employer's competitive position. The 2005 Act on Supervision of Commercial Practices (57/2005) stipulates that a party having obtained knowledge or control of business secrets in a just manner in the course of his work for another or in association with another may not without permission grant information thereon or utilize such secrets. This prohibition remains valid for three years as of the completion of work or the termination of agreement. Furthermore, a party having on account of his work or position in other respects been trusted to retain drawings, descriptions, prescriptions, models or the like is forbidden the utilization thereof or to grant others use thereof without special authority. A third party receiving information or business secrets, in a manner violating provisions of the Act, is not permitted to utilize them. Violations of the Act are subject to fines or imprisonment for up to six months in case of a serious offence.

# Chapter 10. Inventions by Employees

*226.* Although the main principle of Icelandic copyright law stipulates that an author is the owner of any product resulting from his own creation, an employment relationship can have the effect that the copyright transfers to the employer. On the Icelandic labour market it is generally presumed that results of work performed by an employee for the employer belongs to the employer, to the extent necessary for the object of the employment relationship to be reached. Hence, the employer can in many cases exercise the outcome or product in the manner he chooses without the intervention of the employee. However, the general copyright perspectives can come into consideration regarding certain professions. To avoid controversy it is necessary to provide provisions regarding employee inventions in employment contracts in cases where it might be relevant.

# Chapter 11. Settlement of Disputes

*227.* Disputes in the Icelandic labour market can be divided into two separate categories. On the one hand there are disputes relating to the application and interpretation of statutory rights and obligations as well as interpretation, validity and infringement of existing collective agreements. In accordance with the TUI Act, such disputes over legal issues do not validate work stoppage, strikes and lockouts, since if there is a valid agreement between a trade union and employers regarding workers' wages and terms, the right to strike does not exist. On the other, there are wage disputes that arise between trade unions and employees when collective agreements expire or are non-existent. Under such conditions work stoppage, strikes and lockouts can be used by both parties to achieve their objectives. Such conflicts are in general resolved by collective bargaining, sometimes with the assistance of a mediator or a conciliation committee.

*228.* It is of great importance to distinguish between the two categories of dispute since different methods of legal recourse are used to resolve them.

## §1. GRIEVANCE PROCEDURES

*229.* As previously stated, different measures of resolution exist depending on the category of dispute. It furthermore differs what recourses are applicable and most convenient for the disputing parties within each category. Disputes in the labour market are often resolved on the primary stages in an informal manner with a result both parties agree upon. Several resources are available for the disputing parties before an issue is referred to the courts. Collective agreements often include provisions of resolutions that the parties have negotiated upon in case a dispute arises. Such resolutions include agreements to refer disputes to reconciliation committees or arbitration.

## I. Reconciliation Committees

*230.* One of the measures commonly provided for in collective agreements to handle disputes before issues are referred to the courts is reconciliation committees. These provisions either provide for a permanently instated committee which deals with disputes as they arise or the authority to appoint such a committee when and if the occasion arises. Generally both parties to the agreement in question can appoint an individual to the committee and then agree on a third neutral person. A provision regarding a reconciliation committee has by judicial precedent not been considered compulsory in Icelandic labour law, and even when such provisions are present in collective agreements either party can refer the matter of dispute in question to the courts.

## II. Arbitration

*231.* Another measure used to solve disputes in the labour market is the arbitration court (*Gerdardómur*). Parties to collective agreements as well as employment contracts have the right to include in their agreements that disputes, in general or regarding certain defined issues, should be decided upon by an arbitration court according to the rules of the 1989 Act on Contractual Arbitration (53/1989). Parties to an agreement can also decide upon the usage of arbitration after a dispute arises. Disputes that would normally be subject to resolution of the general courts can therefore be resolved by arbitration, provided both parties are in agreement, which is a precondition for the procedure. If a dispute has been brought before general courts which falls under the scope of a valid arbitration agreement the court may only dismiss the case pursuant to a request from one of the parties.

*232.* Rulings of arbitration courts are binding for the parties, although some aspects of the proceedings can be challenged and referred to the general courts. However, an arbitration agreement is not binding if there are material deviations from the formal requirements stipulated in the Act on contractual arbitrations. Furthermore the validity of the decision of an arbitration is conditioned upon the matter being capable of settlement by arbitration and the provisions pertaining to the appointment of arbitrators, the procedure or other provisions in the arbitration agreement providing for adequate judicial protection.

## §2. ROLE OF THE COURTS

*233.* Where conflicts between the parties cannot be resolved with the assistance of reconciliation committees or the parties are not willing to refer matters to such committees, the resolution of the disputes can be directed to the Labour Court or courts of general jurisdiction, depending on the nature of the dispute.

## I. The Labour Court

*234.* The Labour Court was established by the enactment of the TUI Act and is located in Reykjavik. The Labour Court is a special court on labour matters with jurisdiction of the whole country, and as such not a part of the general court system.

*235.* The Court consists of five persons appointed for the term of three years. One is appointed by ASÍ, on by SA, one by the Minister of Welfare out of three persons nominated by the Supreme Court, and two by the Supreme Court, one of whom specially nominated to be the President of the Court. If an employer who is a party to a case before the Court is not a not a member of the SA or an employee is not a member of any trade union or federation of trade unions, the judges nominated by the previously mentioned social partners shall vacate their seat and the parties to the case nominate judges to take their place. The competence requirements for Labour Court judges are that they have to be Icelandic citizens, in charge of their financial affairs and with an unblemished reputation. The two judges appointed by the Supreme Court must have a university degree in law. Furthermore, the Court may at any time seek the opinion of specialists on specific items.

*236.* The sphere of the Labour Court is specified in the TUI Act. According to the Act the main functions carried out by the Labour Court are the following:

- to adjudicate in controversies where the TUI Act has been violated and in cases where a loss has been suffered as a consequence of an illegitimate strike;
- to adjudicate in cases where a contract of employment has been violated or where there is a dispute concerning the interpretation of such an agreement and its validity;
- to adjudicate in controversies between employers and employees, where the parties to the controversy have agreed to refer the case to the Labour Court, with the consent of at least three members of the court.

*237.* In general, confederations of trade unions and employers represent their members before the Labour Court. Associations which are not members of a confederation of trade unions or employers represent themselves before the Labour Court as well as individuals that are not members of any federations or unions. In cases where the relevant social partner refuses to institute litigation on the behalf of one of its member, that respective party can in his or her own capacity institute such a litigation. However, this is conditioned on the submission of proof of the refusal of the relevant social partner.

*238.* The judgments of the Labour Court are determent by plurality of votes and in the case of even votes the President's vote will decide issues. The Court may order parties to pay damages, fines and costs in accordance with customary rules. In determining the amount of damages regard may be had for the culpability of the violation. The judgments and decrees of the Labour Court are subject to execution, and the Court will decide upon the respite for execution. Decisions of the court can generally not be appealed to any other court, so they constitute the final result of the dispute. Following issues can, however, be referred to the Supreme Court:

- a judgment or ruling of dismissal;
- a judgment of invalidation on the grounds that the case does not fall within the jurisdiction of the Labour Court;
- an order on the duty to witness, the swearing of oaths and fines for breaches of court procedure under the TUI Act;
- a decision on the imposition of fines on parties under the TUI Act.

*239.* An appeal must be made within a week of the pronouncement of judgment or decree. It is fairly uncommon for decisions of the Labour Court to be subject to appeal to the Supreme Court, and in most cases the appeals have been raised on the question of the Labour Court's jurisdiction.

## II. Courts of General Jurisdiction

*240.* Labour disputes that do not fall under the scope of the TUI Act fall under the jurisdiction of district courts. The most common form of labour dispute that is referred to the district courts revolves around the individual employment relationship, such as conflicts regarding the payment of wages, the length of sabbaticals or unlawful terminations. Such civil cases are subject to the 1991 Act on Civil Procedure (91/1991).

*241.* Court cases involving violations of the Penal Code or other criminal activity, such as sexual harassment or certain violations of the WEHS Act, are subject to the Code of Criminal Procedure. The legal procedure and investigative methods employed in criminal cases in Iceland are subject to the 2008 Act on Criminal Procedure (88/2008). In these cases the state prosecutor puts forward the charges in the case but complainant is not a party to the court presiding, unlike in civil cases.

# Part II. Collective Labour Relations

## Chapter 1. Trade Union Freedom

### §1. FREEDOM OF ASSOCIATION

*242.* Associations play an important role in Icelandic society; among them are associations of employees, trade unions and associations of employers which work for the joint interest of their members with their activities. The social partners influence the economic life considerably, e.g., by concluding collective agreements which enjoy special protection under the Constitution (Articles 74 and 75).

*243.* The concept of freedom of association is tightly linked with freedom of expression and has been considered to be one of the cornerstones of a democracy. Freedom of association can be considered in two aspects. First there is the freedom to form or join associations, and second the freedom not to join or freely depart from associations. These two factors are intended to protect the individual freedom of choice, but in fact this is a case of joint human rights since the right is only utilized in relations to associations. The freedom of association is protected by the Icelandic Constitution. This fundamental freedom is also protected under international and regional human rights conventions, like Article 11 of the European Convention on Human Rights (ECHR), which has not only been ratified in Iceland but also incorporated into Icelandic legislation (cf. the Act on ECHR (62/1994)).

*244.* The Icelandic Constitution stipulates that associations may be formed without prior permission for any lawful purpose, including political associations and trade unions. An association may not be dissolved by administrative decision (Article 74). The activities of an association found to be in furtherance of unlawful objectives may, however, be enjoined, in which case legal action should be brought without undue delay for a judgment dissolving the association. Article 74 of the Constitution furthermore stipulates that no one may be obliged to be a member of any association. Membership of an association may, however, be made obligatory by law if this is necessary in order to enable an association to discharge its functions in the public interest or on account of the rights of others.

*245.* The original purpose of the constitutional right to freedom of association was mainly to protect the political right of individuals to establish associations, that they would not be obliged to get a special permission from authorities for this purpose and that the operation of associations would not be subject to supervision by authorities. In recent times the emphasis has to some extent shifted to the rights of the associations themselves. This applies in particular to the trade unions and their right to organize their internal affairs without the involvement of the authorities, as well as to negotiate and conclude collective agreements on behalf of their members. Additionally, there has been more emphasis on the negative part of the freedom of association in recent years; the right of individuals not to be members or pay fees to associations they do not wish to adhere to. Human rights conventions protecting the right to freedom of association have had considerable effect in this regard, especially the above-mentioned Article 11 of the ECHR.

*246.* According to Supreme Court case law, trade unions' right to bargain collectively as well as their right to strike is protected under the freedom of association provision of the Constitution. This is, however, not without limitations, but the Court has essentially interpreted those limitations in consensus with the interpretations of the European Court of Human Rights of the European Human Rights Convention, Article 11, and relevant case law.

§2. FREEDOM TO FORM AND JOIN TRADE UNIONS

*247.* Both the Icelandic Constitution and ratified human rights conventions ensure the right to form associations for any lawful purpose, including trade unions, as well as joining them without special permission or intervention of the government. The authorities are thus prohibited from interfering with the establishment of unions as well as the activities carried out within them, provided their actions and objectives are lawful in nature. Despite this, the government can concern itself with issues relating to the establishment of associations with legislation regarding certain aspects, such as official registration and official monitoring, provided these obligations do not constitute a hindrance of the intended role of the association. The freedom of association without the interference of the government does not therefore prevent the legislators from requiring associations to meet certain conditions to gain legal status: This has, however, limited relevance with regard to trade unions, since they are not obliged to register or be subject to public monitoring under Icelandic law.

*248.* Trade unions and political associations are mentioned specifically in the freedom of association provision of the Constitution and are considered to enjoy special constitutional protection as such. The TUI Act includes rules on trade union activities, such as procedures in cases of work stoppage and resolution of disputes arising from violations of the Act and the interpretation of collective agreements. The fundamental rule of trade union freedom is affirmed in the first article of the Act, where it is stated that people have the right to establish trade unions and trade union confederations in order to collaborate in the interests of the working class and workers in general.

*249.* The principle of trade union independence is put forward in the TUI Act, where it is stated that the unions are in charge of their own affairs within the restrictions set by the Act. This autonomy of the unions entails that they themselves provide the rules and framework around their activities, including conditions and requirements regarding certain qualifications of their members. This freedom is however limited by provisions in the TUI Act, stating that trade unions are required to be open to all workers belonging to the relevant trade within the operating district of the trade union concerned (Article 2).

§3. Freedom Not to Join Trade Unions

*250.* Prior to 1995 Icelandic courts had taken a clear position that the scope of the freedom of association provision of the Constitution did not entail protection of the right not to join associations. Following the ECHR judgment in the case of *Sigurdur Sigurjónsson v. Iceland* in 1993, the provision was changed in 1995. The second paragraph of the freedom of association provision in the Constitution now states that no one may be obliged to be a member of an association. Membership may, however, be obligatory by law if it is necessary in order to enable an association to discharge its functions in the public interest or on account of the rights of others.

*251.* In this context, questions have arisen concerning the legitimacy of so-called priority clauses in collective agreements, which stipulate that members of a particular union shall be given priority regarding employment. Furthermore, questions have been raised regarding the payment of workers to trade unions irrespective of membership. According to the WTP Act (Article 6:2) an employer must withhold from his employee's wages union contributions in accordance with the relevant collective agreement. Additionally, the CAPS Act (Article 7:2) states that public servants are to pay union fees regardless of union membership in accordance with the relevant collective agreement, provided that wages and other benefits are based on that same agreement.

*252.* It should, however, be mentioned that when changing the freedom of association provision of the Constitution, the legislator did not aspire to affect the situation on the labour market with regard to priority clauses and obligatory union fees. On that basis Icelandic courts have determined that such provisions are not in conflict with the freedom of association provision. However, it has to be considered likely with respect to the interpretation of ECHR (Article 11) that in at least some instances the right to remain outside a union is being violated under the current practice.

# Chapter 2. Trade Unions and Employers' Associations

## §1. Concept and Degree of Organization

*253.* The Icelandic labour market is for the most part regulated by collective bargaining, and in Icelandic enterprises collective relations focus on the relationship between the trade union and the employer. There is no general definition of either a trade union or an employers' association in Icelandic law, but the TUI Act stipulates the right to establish trade unions and confederations of trade unions for the purpose of working jointly for the interests of the working class and wage earners in general.

*254.* As previously covered in paragraphs 242–245, the fundamental rule of freedom of association is guaranteed in the Icelandic Constitution. The labour market associations are free voluntary associations, developed on democratic principles. They are in charge of their own affairs, including the union statutes, subject to the limitations imposed in the aforementioned TUI Act. The Act therefore creates the framework of the labour market, but the rights that the legislation provides are further elaborated and put into force by labour market associations, the social partners, on behalf of their members.

*255.* The general level of unionization is high in Iceland, about 85%, lowest in financial and company services but highest among general workers, seamen and in the public service.

## §2. Trade Unions

### I. Role

*256.* As stated above, the primary purpose of employee organizations is to work jointly for the interests of the working class and wage earners in general. Their main role is to draw up collective agreements on wages and wage-related issues and put them into operation. It is not only members of trade unions who benefit from collective agreements as in Iceland wages and other working terms in collective agreements are considered minimum terms for all wage earners in the relevant occupation within the area covered by the agreement, regardless of their union membership. Besides this, one of the main functions of trade unions is to take care of the interests and rights of their members in relation to employers and their organizations and in relation to the government and public services. Unions therefore also have the role of ensuring that their members are receiving their negotiated rights and assisting members in cases of grievances against employers.

*257.* During the early years of trade unions in Iceland, the main objectives were gaining recognition of employers as well as the government, of the right to negotiate on the behalf of their members, that wages were paid according to the union scale, that the priority of work by union members would be respected and the right of all workers to unionize. Unions in Iceland have over the years fought to achieve just compensation for their members, remuneration in the form of salaries, social security, vacation time and so forth. Development in these areas has often been in such a way that individual trade unions have gained a variety of rights for their members through collective bargaining, and legislation has followed later. There is a long-standing tradition of a multiple social role of trade unions in Iceland. From the beginning, the scope of trade union negotiation has included pensions, housing, social security, vacation housing, health and security in the workplace and education. To this effect trade unions are considered authorized to collect funds and allocate them for the purpose of benefiting their members.

## II. Structure

*258.* As stated above, the TUI Act lays down the general framework of the labour market and defines the role and obligations of trade unions. However, the structure of unions is not specifically regulated by law although the general applications of corporate law (*félagaréttur*) apply to their formation, structure and dissolution.

*259.* The first trade unions in Iceland were established shortly before the turn of the twentieth century. The initiative was taken by printers, who are believed to have established the first trade union of craftsmen in 1887. However, an association of workers and seamen had been established earlier but was both different in nature and proved to be short-lived. Today the union structure in Iceland is essentially based on trade or profession and operates either on a national or local level. In most cases the unions are members of an umbrella organization which may involve a multiplicity of unions. Over the years the development has been that trade unions have merged and expanded in the line with the expansion of municipalities since union regions cannot be smaller than the municipality they operate in. This expansion has furthermore been influenced by a willingness to promote and increase the influence of the unions.

### A. The Icelandic Confederation of Labour

*260.* In 1916 the existing trade unions formed an umbrella organization, ASÍ, which to this day is the largest confederation of workers in Iceland. ASÍ was equally a political party, at that time named the People's Party, now the Social Democratic Party. ASÍ was to take responsibility for agreements with employers concerning pay and working conditions, while the People's Party was to promote the general and economic interests of the working class in the political arena. In the long run this dual role proved troublesome, with the result that the two bodies split in 1940.

*261.* ASÍ is the largest federation of workers in Iceland with a membership count of over 130,000, which amounts to about two-thirds of the national labour force. ASÍ is made up of forty-eight trade unions of general workers, office and retail workers, seamen, construction and industrial workers, electrical workers and various other professions. These trade unions are affiliated to five national federations, which in turn are affiliated to ASÍ. In addition there are seven national unions directly affiliated to ASÍ. The two largest trade unions in Iceland are (1) the Efling Trade Union with approximately 27,000 members and (2) the VR Trade Union with approximately 30,000 members. Trade unions belonging to ASÍ represent almost exclusively workers in the private sector, but some of their members are also employed by the state and municipal authorities.

262. The role of ASÍ is to promote the interests of its constituent federations, trade unions and workers by providing leadership through coordination of policies in the fields of employment, social, education, environment and labour market issues. ASÍ represents the trade union movement at various levels of interaction with the government on issues such as labour law, employment and social policy, vocational education and training and occupational safety.

263. The supreme power in the affairs of ASÍ is held by the confederation's annual meeting where 290 elected representatives of employees nationwide gather. Every member union has the right to send at least one representative, irrespective of the relevant union's size. The annual meeting of ASÍ decides on the policy of the confederation, and its leadership is elected. The central control board of ASÍ consists of fifteen representatives who are responsible for the daily administration and management between the annual meetings. On the behalf of the central control board a range of subsidiary committees are operated which focus on specified categories. These specialized committees have an important role as a place of dialogue and development within ASÍ. The association's policymaking is mainly formed on the basis of the work done in these committees and then put into force by the central control board.

## B.  Trade Unions Outside Union Associations

264. Although most trade unions in the private sector are members of ASÍ, there are some that have chosen to stand outside the confederation and the national associations within ASÍ. These unions are, however, relatively few and make up only a small part of the labour market. Among the largest of these trade unions are the Icelandic Nurses' Association, the Icelandic Union of Foremen and Supervisors and the Icelandic Engineering Union.

## C.  Public Sector Unions

265. Over the years the situation on the labour market has been quite different when it comes to public sector employees. In the year 1962 the public sector was granted limited rights to collective bargaining but until then their pay was determined by special laws. The right to collective bargaining is, however, much more restricted than in the private sector (*see* further review regarding these limitations in

paragraphs 352–353). Employees in the public sector are organized into various unions, which belong to three different confederations: (1) the Confederation of Workers of the State and Communities (BSRB), (2) the Confederation of Academic Workers (BHM) and (3) the Teachers Union (KÍ).

## D. The Confederation of Workers of the State and Communities

266. BSRB was founded in 1942 and is the largest union of employees in public services. BSRB is grouped into twenty-five member unions with approximately 21,000 members, of which two-thirds are women. The union members work in the fields of customs, police, fire resistance, healthcare, education of preschool children, etc. BSRB members are employed by both municipalities as well as the state.

## E. The Association of Academics

267. BHM was founded in 1958 and is an umbrella organization for trade unions of academics. To be admitted to one of the member unions an applicant must have completed a university programme of at least three years' duration. There are twenty-six member unions in BHM, consisting of around 13,000 employees. Most of BHM's members are employed by the state, municipalities or other public entities. The private sector has, however, in the last few years increasingly employed academics from BHM ranks. The member unions themselves preserve the right to negotiate collective agreements for their members, but BHM assists the member unions in many fields and speaks for academics in common causes.

## F. The Icelandic Teachers' Union

268. KÍ was founded in the year 2000 and is a joint organization for all teachers, head teachers, deputy head teachers and student counsellors, in preschools, primary schools, secondary schools and music schools, with the exception of head teachers in secondary schools. KÍ has eight member associations. The individual member associations work independently, negotiating wage contracts for their members. KÍ, however, works towards rights and interests that are common to all members, such as pensions, sick leave and parental leave.

## III. Rule of Membership

269. As mentioned above, trade unions have in general the power to conduct their own affairs, within the limits laid down by law. There are, however, some aspects of trade union activities that are laid down in law by the TUI Act. The chief of these rules is that the union's area of operation may not be smaller than the local municipality it operates in, and the unions must be open to everyone in the relevant field of employment. As described above, a very high proportion of employees in

Iceland, approximately 85%, are unionized. Historically, this high proportion is doubtless due to the existence of so-called priority provisions by which the employers give a legal undertaking to provide union members with precedence for work; in return the union is obliged to admit a non-union member whom an employer wishes to engage. In the past some collective agreements went even further, with obligatory membership provisions, under which all employees covered by the agreement were expressly obliged to be members of a specific trade union. However, today there are very few, if any, examples of this in Iceland. The arrangement has been regarded as unconstitutional following the enactment in 1995 of a provision in the second paragraph of Article 74 of the Constitution, stating that no person may be obliged to be a member of an association. On the other hand, Icelandic courts have viewed priority provisions as compatible with this constitutional provision. The distinction between obligatory membership provisions and priority provisions is not one of long-standing in Iceland. It resulted from the aforementioned amendment to the Constitution in 1995. Following this, ASÍ amended its statutes, which now state that the statutes of its constituent unions may not contain provisions on obligatory membership. Laws and collective agreements also contain terms which oblige employers to collect union subscriptions and pass them to trade unions. According to the WTP Act, an employer is obliged to deduct from an employee's wages his contributions to the relevant trade union, if applicable, according to rules set forth in collective agreements.

270. According to the CAPS Act, trade unions in the public sector have to meet certain criteria in order to obtain the right to bargain collectively. In fact matters in the public sector are organized rather differently from in the private sector. The Act stipulates that only one trade union shall have the right to negotiate agreements with the same employer for the same class of employees. Collective agreements of public servants do not contain priority clauses nor are there any examples of clauses obliging employees to join a trade union. Employees working for the state or local authorities have a right to join a union, and also the right not to join a union, cf. the constitutional rule discussed above. However, as mentioned above, those standing outside of unions still have to pay a subscription as if they were members of the relevant union.

271. As stated above, the fundamental rule is that trade unions are to be open to all those belonging to the trade concerned within the district of each union in accordance with further fixed rules contained in their statutes (Article 2 of the TUI Act). In general, all limitations to the right of employees to become members of trade unions have to be objective, based on the purpose of the union and in no way discriminatory. It is generally accepted that any restrictions regarding union membership should be interpreted narrowly, in view of the importance the union membership can have for employees in relations to priority clauses for example. Such restrictions can, however, be permitted by special legal provisions and in some instances developed through case law.

## IV. Lawful Restrictions

### A. *Education and Qualifications*

*272.* Trade unions are permitted to include provisions in their laws or statutes regarding specific education or qualification requirements of their members. Access to these unions is therefore exclusive to those workers meeting the specific requirements.

### B. *Profession*

*273.* Trade unions are permitted to limit their membership to a certain profession. Such restrictions have been considered legitimate in Iceland, but when a dispute arises as to whether a certain employee belongs to a particular profession, the Labour Court has interpreted such provisions broadly.

### C. *Age*

*274.* Age requirements for union membership can either be in regard to minimum age for admission or maximum age. As a general rule in Iceland, trade unions require their members to have attained the age of 16. Provisions regarding the maximum age of union members are not common but have been considered legitimate.

### D. *Unpaid Union Fees*

*275.* According to ASÍ's statutes, no member union can accept a member who is in debt to another member union or has been dismissed from a member union unless the board of the former union approves it (Article 7). The legitimacy of the provision has not been argued in Icelandic courts in spite of criticism that it deprives people of the fundamental human right of union membership on the grounds of a capital claim from a third party.

## V. Unlawful Restrictions

### A. *Residence*

*276.* Restrictions on union membership based on residence or legal residence are unlawful in Iceland, and union statutes cannot include provisions thereon.

## B. Nationality

277. Restrictions on union membership based on nationality are in all cases unlawful in Iceland.

## C. Gender

278. Any restrictions on union membership based on gender as well as any discrimination, whether direct or indirect, is unlawful in Iceland (cf. the Gender Equality Act). Furthermore the Act stipulates that employers and trade unions have the obligation to work systematically towards the goal of gender equality in the workplace (Article 18 of the Gender Equality Act).

## D. Membership of Another Trade Union

279. According to case law set forward by the Labour Court, it is unlawful for trade unions to refuse to grant membership on the basis that the worker in question is already a member of another union.

## VI. Withdrawal from Trade Unions

280. A member of a trade union ceases to be bound by its statutes at the time he withdraws from the union in question (cf. the TUI Act, Article 3:2). However, the worker will nevertheless be bound by the provisions of the unions' relevant collective agreement during the duration of its validity. This rule has been confirmed in numerous judgments of the Labour Court, based on the assumption that a worker cannot unilaterally change the collective basis of wages and other benefits of a mutual agreement during the contract period. The TUI Act therefore provides workers with the right to withdraw from a trade union but leaves the authority to implement the rules of procedures regarding withdrawal to the trade unions themselves. According to the TUI Act and case law, unions can put restrictions on the withdrawal of their members, provided that such restrictions are objective and do not go further than necessary. Furthermore, such restrictions are always reviewed with regard to the principle of freedom of association, which specifically protects the right of workers to remain outside unions.

## VII. Rights and Duties of Trade Union Members

281. The TUI Act specifically stipulates that trade union members shall be protected from penalization due to their union membership and forbids employers and their representatives from attempting to influence their employees' dealings with

trade unions and industrial disputes. Most trade unions statutes contain terms on the rights and duties of their members. In general, they are guaranteed the following rights:

- to work under the terms and conditions as agreed upon in the relevant collective agreement;
- freedom of expression as well as entitlement to propose motions and vote at unions meetings;
- to be eligible as candidates in elections for shop stewards;
- to grants from union funds;
- to receive support from the trade union against employers who fail to observe contracts and laws of the labour market;
- to appeal in cases of violations of union members.

The main duties of trade union members are:

- to obey the statutes of the relevant union, motions agreed at union meetings and all agreements of the union;
- to pay their union fees promptly;
- to carry out tasks of representation of their union and to refuse to work with non-union staff and inform the union if they become aware that this is happening;
- in some cases union statutes also contain provisions stipulating that union members have the duty to encourage non-union members to join the union.

## VIII. Penalties for Violations

*282.* Individual union members are bound by the union's legally constituted agreements and contracts (cf. the TUI Act, Article 3:1). The provision is given additional weight by penalty clauses in the Act, laying down fines and compensation if the statutes are not obeyed. In addition, most trade union statutes and agreements include provisions regarding penalties in cases of violation by members. A union member who fails to follow the union rules faces demands for damages, fines or expulsion from the union. However, the interests of a worker to be a member to a union are significant and expulsion from the union can lead to great inconvenience, for example refusal of admission to another union. Therefore strict demands are made regarding the legitimacy of expulsion and the severity of the reasons leading to such a measure being taken. A member can generally challenge such penalties during a trade union annual meeting, according to most union statutes. Additionally, it has to be considered certain that Icelandic courts would enforce provisions on expulsion with the greatest caution and only in case of serious breaches, but no case law has been established regarding these matters.

§3. Employers' Associations

*283.* The initiative of forming employers' organizations in Iceland was taken by trawler owners, who established an association in 1916, which over the following decades became the chief spokesman for employers. However, no overall employers' association was established until 1934, which at that time was, however, far from extending to all employers on the labour market.

*284.* The Icelandic employer's organization (VSÍ) was established in 1934. In 1999 the organization merged with the Employers' Union of Cooperatives (VMSS) in forming Confederation of Icelandic Employers (SA).

*285.* SA is a service organization which represents and promotes the views of employers and offers services in numerous areas to Icelandic businesses. SA projects include negotiations of collective agreements with unions on wages and working conditions, to advocate for an internationally competitive legal and regulatory environment as well as the interpretation and communication of decisions by government authorities that directly affect the business environment. SA furthermore employs specialists who provide members with a variety of services, information and advice.

*286.* In addition, SA has clear political objectives regarding the labour market and continuously advocates on issues like a competitive tax regime, a flexible labour market and minimal regulatory burden.

*287.* SA and its member associations include about 2,000 businesses and account for about 50% of all salaried employees on the Icelandic labour market. The confederation, on the behalf of its members associations, enters into agreement with 95% of employees on the private labour market. SA constitutes a comprehensive Confederation of Icelandic Employers that combines the forces of its eight member associations. A business becomes a member of SA by joining one of the six member associations and thus holds dual membership status. SA members associations are:

- the Association of Financial Institutions in Iceland (SFF);
- the Federation of district heating, electric utilities and waterworks (Samorka);
    the Federation of Trade and Services(SVTH);
- the Federation of Icelandic Industries (SI);
- the Icelandic Travel Industry Association (SAF);
- Fisheries Iceland (SFS).

*288.* By becoming members of SA, the member associations grant the Confederation a mandate to represent them in wage negotiations and for entering into decisions regarding work stoppages.

*289.* When joining SA, the member associations and individual enterprises furthermore become obliged to abide by the provisions of the confederation statutes, as well as decisions based on them. The members of SA are free to organize in local employers' associations whose primary goal is to promote the special interests of employers in the relevant area. The eight SA member associations operate on the basis of the different industrial activities involved, and each of them has the initiative in its own matters within the separate industrial sphere.

*290.* The three main bodies of SA are (1) the Board of Directors, (2) the Board of Representatives and (3) the executive board. However, the annual meeting of the Confederation holds the supreme power in the affairs of SA. The annual meeting is held before the end of May every year and must be called at least four weeks in advance by means of a notification to the members. The right to attend the annual meeting with the freedom of speech and proposal is held by the management of the member enterprises, other members and the employees of SA, and the member associations.

*291.* The chairman of SA is elected annually in a direct open postal election of all members. The vice-chairman is, however, elected from among the members of the Board of Directors at the first meeting of the Board after the annual meeting.

*292.* The Board of Representatives of SA holds the supreme power in the affairs of the Confederation between its annual meetings. The role of the Board of Representatives is to elect annually the twenty-member board of directors and to assist it in formulating SA's strategies as determined by the Board at any given time. The eight SA member associations annually distribute among themselves the hundred seats on the SA board of representatives unless businesses opt to claim their seats on the Board directly.

*293.* The Confederation's Board of Directors formulates its strategy and focal points. The Board of Directors holds quarterly meetings or more often if so requested by at least two board members. Eligible on the Board of Directors are the management and board members of the member enterprises and the member associations.

*294.* The Confederation's Executive Board is elected by the Board of Directors at the first board meeting held after the annual meeting. The Executive Board consists of the Confederation's chairman and vice-chairman and five persons whom the Board elects among the board members. The Executive Board supervises SA's activities in accordance with the strategy of the Board of Directors and the annual meeting. Decisions, which the Executive Board is expected to make according to these statutes, may also be made by the Board of SA.

## Chapter 3. Institutionalized Relations

*295.* Institutionalized relations between employers and employees in Iceland are quite limited. This is for many reasons; the economic environment in Iceland has been largely made up of small- and medium-sized enterprises (SMEs) with the result that informal channels are very important. Social dialogue mechanisms have a long tradition on the Icelandic labour market, partly based on the TUI Act. On the other, direct consultation within Icelandic companies between owners and their employees is a fairly recent development. There are some forms of institutionalized relations which are bound by law in Iceland, which in many cases stem from EU directives that have been transposed into Icelandic law. Most of these rules have, however, only relatively limited relevance on the Icelandic labour market.

*296.* Union representatives in Iceland, a general system of worker representation at the workplace, has existed since 1938, established under the TUI Act and further developed in collective agreements. Union representatives are nominated under the TUI Act (Article 9) and collective agreements. This rule does not, however, extend to agricultural workers or the crews of vessels or boats. In a workplace where there are five–fifty employees they are entitled to elect one union representative from their group. If there are fifty workers or more, two union representatives may be elected. After the election the relevant trade union nominates the union representative(s) for the position and reports the election to the leaders of the company. If it is not possible to elect a union representative, he shall be nominated by the trade union but then his term of office shall be no longer than two years.

*297.* In general if many trade unions represent workers at a single working place, each of them has their representative there. However, at smaller working places, where members of more than one union work together, the workers elect one representative who represents all of them. Where a dispute arises between trade unions as to which of them shall appoint a trade union representative, ASÍ decides on the issue.

*298.* According to the TUI Act the role of union representatives is to monitor that work agreements are adhered to by the employer and his representatives and that the employees' social or civil rights are not curtailed. The law gives union representatives two additional prerogatives: (1) supervision and (2) handling of complaints. Employees should address their complaints about the employer and/or his representatives to their trade union representative. As soon as a union representative has received a complaint from an employee or he considers himself to have a reason for assuming that the right of an employee or a trade union official at his work station has been infringed by the employer or his representative, he must forthwith investigate the matter. If he comes to the conclusion that the complaints or his suspicion have been substantiated, he should approach the employer or his representative with a complaint and demand amendment. The union representative should furthermore as soon as possible must send a report to the trade union about the employee's complaints as well as making a report stating what an employer or his representatives are considered to have violated against employees and their unions

(Article 10 of the TUI Act). Trade union representatives are assigned additional tasks by legislation, like the 2006 Information and Consultation Act (151/2006) discussed below, collective agreements and trade union statutes. As representatives of the trade union at the workplace they act as contact persons between the union and employers.

*299.* Special protection is granted to union representatives by the TUI Act, whereas employers and their representatives are not permitted to terminate their employment on account of their service as such or to allow them in any way to suffer for the fact that a trade union has charged them with discharging union representative's duties for the union. Where employers are required to reduce the number of employees a union representative shall, other things being equal, have priority in retaining employment. In accordance with general collective agreements, shop stewards are permitted in consultation with the relevant trade union and the management of the workplace, to call a meeting with employees twice a year during working hours at the workplace. Furthermore, a union representative is entitled, after consulting his employer, to leave work on account of his duties as shop steward without any reduction of wages (Article 11).

*300.* The executive committee of the trade union concerned is authorized to deprive a shop steward of his commission and nominate another person, if in its judgment the shop steward has neglected his duties in accordance with the TUI Act (Article 12).

*301.* For the public sector, provisions concerning union representatives are in the 1986 CAPS Act.

*302.* The union representatives are virtually the sole representatives of workers. However, according to legislation deriving from the EEA Agreement, which grants employees the right to information and consultation under certain conditions, if the trade unions are not represented by a trade union representative, they are entitled to choose their joint representative instead, as under the 2000 Collective Redundancies Act. In other cases, if there is no union representative at the workplace, workers shall be informed and consulted under the law (cf. the 2002 Transfer of Undertakings Act).

## I. Health and Safety in the Workplace

*303.* The 1980 WEHS Act covers certain aspects of the employer–employee relationship in the workplace. The Act dictates that employers with one–nine employees must work towards a good working environment, and health and safety at the workplace, in close cooperation with the employees of the enterprise and their trade union representative (Article 4). According to the Act, employers who employ ten people or more must appoint one person as a safety guard on their behalf and employees should appoint another from their group as a safety representative

(Article 5). Their role is to work cooperatively to ensure that the working environment, health and safety at the workplace are in accordance with the WEHS Act.

*304.* In a workplace employing more than fifty people, a safety committee must be established. Employees select two representatives from their group, and the employer appoints two additional representatives (Article 6 of the WEHS Act). The role of the committee is to organize activities concerning the working environment, health and safety within the workplace, to inform the employees on relevant matters, to conduct inspections at the workplace and to ensure that measures taken to improve the working environment, health and safety are fully effective.

*305.* The employer is obliged to appoint a representative to the safety committee with full powers if he himself is not a member of the committee. The employer must furthermore promote the cooperation of those elected to deal with working conditions, health and safety in the workplaces and those who are in charge of health services and the protection of workers' health. In addition the employer must guarantee that those elected to deal with working conditions, health and safety in the workplace and those who are members of the safety committee are allocated appropriate time to attend to their duties as well as ensuring that they have the opportunity to acquire necessary knowledge and education concerning issues relating to those duties. Nominated parties also have a right to all information concerning working environment, health and safety in the workplace that relates to them performing their duties (Article 8 of the WEHS Act).

*306.* The employer or his representative, the safety representative of the employees, their trade union representative and the safety committees where they are operated are to be contacted when employees of AOSH inspect workplaces. The named parties shall be assisted as much as possible in bringing their problems to AOSH (Article 6:2 of the WEHS Act).

## II. Information and Consultation

*307.* The 2006 Act on Information and Consultation in Undertakings (151/2006) implemented Directive 2002/14/EC that established a general framework for informing and consulting employees in the European Community. The Act applies to undertakings in which an average of at least fifty persons are employed in the domestic labour market. It does not apply to the crews of ocean-going vessels. In the legislative documents of the Act it is stipulated that as the Act applies to diverse companies, both in the private and public sector, further procedures in this regard will depend on collective agreements or agreements between employers and workers' representatives. Its aim is to guarantee the right of employees to information and consultation in undertakings and to encourage employees' representatives and undertakings to work in a spirit of cooperation when structuring and implementing their mechanisms for information and consultation, taking the interests of both parties into account.

*308.* The Act assumes that union representatives will play a major role as employee representatives with regard to information and consultation. Furthermore, those employees who are not represented by union representatives should have a common representative to serve in this capacity. The Act allows for the adoption of another arrangement through collective agreements as well as an agreement on a different application or a method which has been practised within a company (Article 3:1).

*309.* Employers should provide employees' representatives with information concerning the following: (a) recent developments and the outlook concerning the undertaking's activities and financial standing; (b) the situation, structure and outlook regarding employment in the undertaking, and all foreseeable measures, particularly where a threat to job security is involved; and (c) decisions that are likely to lead to substantial changes in the structure of work or employees' employment contracts, including decisions that are based on the provisions of the Changes of Ownership of Undertakings Act and the Collective Redundancies Act (Article 4). Following on the providing of information under items (b) and (c) above, the employees' representatives shall be given an opportunity for consultation by meeting the employer and obtaining a response to any opinion that they may express. Furthermore, the employer should explain to the employees' representatives his reasons for that response. Consultation regarding decisions under item (c) above should take place with a view to reaching an agreement on the decisions (Article 5). Employers are not obliged to provide employees' representatives with information or to engage in consultation with them if the information is, according to objective criteria, of such a nature that it might cause serious damage or disturbance to the activities of the undertaking (Article 7). Employees' representatives and any experts who assist them may be bound by confidentiality if this is in the legitimate interest of the undertaking (Article 8). Violations of the Act are subject to penalties (Article 10).

*310.* Under the Act, provisions may be made, e.g., in collective agreements on the structure and implementation of mechanism for information and consultation within undertakings; as appropriate, deviations may be made from the provisions concerning information and consultation (Articles 4 and 5), provided that the aim of the Act is observed (Article 6). Collective agreements in the private sector, between ASÍ and SA, from 2008 include a protocol on the arrangement of information and consultation in companies, with reference to the 2006 Information and Consultation Act. According to the protocol collaboration committees with two employee representatives and two employer's representatives should be established. Their main objective is to receive information and undertake consultations under the Act. These committees have still not been established and neither the Act nor the collective agreements have therefore come fully into effect. It is therefore not possible to assert that the directive or the Act/collective agreements have yet promoted social dialogue between management and labour in Iceland or made sure that employees receive information and are consulted in line with the directive. In this regard the traditions of consultation through informal channels in Icelandic enterprises, which by large are either small- or medium-sized, have to be kept in mind, as described above.

### III. European Work Councils

*311.* The 1999 Act on European Work Councils (61/1999) applies to undertakings and groups of undertakings with at least 1,000 workers in their service in EEA, including at least 150 employees in two establishments in at least two EEA states. The Act implements Council Directive 94/45/EC and aims to improve the right of information and consultation of employees in cases of undertaking or groups of undertakings. Under the Act, workers of undertakings that fall under these specifications are given the right of access to the same information and have the same right as their colleagues within the undertaking or groups of undertakings in other EEA states and to express their points of view to the principal management of the undertaking.

*312.* The central management is responsible for creating the conditions and means necessary for the setting up of a European Works Council or an information and consultation procedure (Article 9 of the Act). The central management shall also initiate the arrangement of a special negotiating body, for the purpose of establishing a works council or rules on information and consultation (Articles 10–11). The special negotiating body and the central management are to work in a spirit of cooperation at the conclusion of a written agreement on the establishment of a works council or rules on information and consultation, and may in this regard be assisted by experts (Article 12).

*313.* Members of the special negotiating body and the works councils as well as the employee representatives shall neither be dismissed from their positions nor suffer any abridgement of their wages or terms of service due to their work. Representatives of employees furthermore enjoy the same sort of legal protection as shop stewards do under the TUI Act. An agreement should be made with the employer guaranteeing employees' representatives the right to take time off work in order to attend properly to their duties under the Act (Article 31).

*314.* It should, however, be noted that very few enterprises in Iceland fall under the scope of the Act on European Work Councils; hence, the provisions in the Act have little relevance to the Icelandic labour market.

### IV. Employees' Representation in Corporate Bodies

*315.* Employees in Iceland are normally not entitled to representation on the boards of companies and nor is there a custom of such arrangement. The only exemption from this is under legislation concerning workers' involvement under EU directives which have been transposed into Icelandic law. These are: the 2004 Act on the involvement of employees in European Companies (27/2004), the 2007 Act concerning involvement of employees in European Cooperative Societies (44/2007) and the 2009 Act concerning involvement of employees in cross-border mergers of limited liability companies (86/2009). The content of these Acts, which follow closely the provisions of the relevant directives, is very similar.

# Chapter 4. Collective Bargaining

## §1. The Collective Bargaining System

*316.* Collective bargaining in Iceland is usually in the form of centralized bargaining involving the employees and employers confederations in the private and public sector and the state/local government. These are so-called national multi-industry negotiations, where the framework and the assumptions for negotiations are decided by the central organizations, and within this framework certain tasks are dealt with at more decentralized level. In recent times the bargaining structure has been shifting towards more company-level bargaining. In general, collective agreements made between trade unions and employers or their organizations are solely made within the relevant occupations.

*317.* As previously explained most trade unions in Iceland are rather small but have grouped together to form larger umbrella organizations, either on a national, regional or sectoral basis. The trade unions are the proper legal contracting partners to negotiate and conclude collective agreements for their members but can transfer the right to make agreements to larger associations. On the employer's side the legal partner of a collective agreement is the single employer, which can equally transfer his right to a larger association of employers. It may therefore vary from time to time which social partners participate in the bargaining process.

*318.* Since the last decade of the twentieth century the national federations within ASÍ have in general negotiated and made collective agreements on behalf of their member unions. This has not, however, been formalized so they have to renew their mandate from the individual member unions for each negotiating round; hence, the association's mandate clearly states that ASÍ is only permitted to negotiate on matters pre-approved in a special contract with its member unions.

*319.* Since 2007 an agreement has been in force between the member unions of ASÍ about which matters shall be dealt with by the confederation. ASÍ has thus in recent years possessed the authority to negotiate the framework of collective agreements and related issues with both SA and the government. On the employer's side, by becoming members of SA, which accounts for about 50% of all salaried employees in the Icelandic labour market, employers have in all general terms transferred their bargaining rights to the association. This does not, however, apply to the entities which are in SA's association divisions, which retain the right to bargain for themselves.

*320.* The government has since the middle of the last century exerted a major influence in the conclusion of collective agreements. Hence, collective agreements in Iceland have on some levels been based on a tripartite consultation, where the government facilitates agreements by introducing economic and social measures in connection with their conclusion. It should however be emphasized here that this practice has not been formalized; its degree varies from time to time, and the government does not become an official member of the collective agreements.

*321.* The fundamental legislation governing the collective bargaining system on the Icelandic labour market is the TUI Act. In the public sector the CAPS Act applies and a special legislation applies to collective agreements in state-owned banks (34/1977). In all sectors of the labour market the fundamental rule regarding the legally binding effects of collective agreements applies. Thus, workers can negotiate for better wages and terms than stipulated in collective agreements, but all agreements which include lesser rights than the relevant collective agreement are by law invalid, regardless of the worker's union membership status.

### §2. COLLECTIVE AGREEMENTS

*322.* The right to bargain collectively is protected by the Icelandic Constitution (Article 75), according to which the right of people to negotiate terms of employment and other labour-related matters shall be regulated by law, as well as the freedom of association provision of Article 74 (*see* paragraphs 242–252). Iceland is also a member of international conventions which protect the right to bargain collectively, for example the European Social Charter and the ILO Right to Organize and Collective Bargaining Convention No. 98 (1949).

*323.* At the beginning of the last century, trade unions often issued unilateral wage rates where a certain minimum salary was stipulated. This changed over time, and in 1938 the right to bargain collectively and the right to strike were first legally ensured in Iceland by the TUI Act. The Act, which has been amended a number of times, empowers trade unions to negotiate agreements with employers concerning wages and other terms of employment of their members. The Act is very focused on trade unions and rarely mentions employers. Its provisions do, however, apply to employers and their associations as appropriate. The TUI Act includes provisions covering the form of collective agreements, on their approval and period of application, the authority of negotiating committees, on workplace agreements, formalities for the giving of notice of termination as well as a schedule for the conduct of negotiations on the renewal of collective agreements. The bargaining structure is on the other hand not regulated by the Act and can be different from one time to another, in particular due to the fact that the bargaining right is in the hands of the single trade unions.

### I. What is a Collective Agreement?

*324.* It is a principle under Icelandic law that contracts do not need to be formalized. The TUI Act contains a deviation from this principle since it stipulates that collective agreements shall be in writing (Article 6). This has not, however, been interpreted strictly by the Labour Court. The term 'collective agreement' is not defined by law, but according to the TUI Act as well as case law it is clear that besides the requirement of a written form, a trade union has to be a member of an agreement if it is to be considered as a collective agreement. On the basis of this a collective agreement can be defined as a written contract made between a trade union on the one hand and an employer, association of employers or confederation of employers on the other, concerning wages and terms of employment, which covers all employees working in the association area of the trade union.

## II. Parties to a Collective Agreement and Its Entry into Force

*325.* As mentioned above, the power to negotiate and make collective agreements is vested with the trade unions, but they can transfer their right as a whole or partly to larger associations, such as national, regional or sectoral organizations or a joint negotiating committee acting on behalf of a number of trade unions. An agreement of such transfer is always made concurrently for approval by the members of the relevant trade unions.

*326.* In general a negotiating committee or representative acts on behalf of the contracting party when a collective agreement is made. These shall in general have a mandate to present proposals for an agreement, take part in negotiations and sign collective agreements on behalf of the trade union or federation involved. Negotiating committees may grant a joint negotiating committee of several unions or federations a mandate to negotiate, in part or completely. A negotiating committee may also require a joint ballot by the members of the unions concerned, in accordance with what the committee may decide at any given time or what may be agreed on in the collective agreements (Article 5:1 of the TUI Act).

*327.* Individual unions may withdraw from the negotiating process at any point during negotiations after delegating their powers to negotiate. As an example, the members of each individual trade union within ASÍ have the unequivocal power to approve or reject collective agreements in each individual case. When the outcome of negotiations is known, a vote is taken in each individual union separately to decide on whether or not that union will be bound by the agreement.

*328.* When a collective agreement has been signed by the competent representatives of the contracting parties, it is valid from the date of signature unless otherwise agreed, unless it is rejected in a secret ballot by a majority of the votes cast, with the participation of at least one-fifth of those on the voting roll or membership register within four weeks of the date of signature. If a general secret postal ballot is held among the members concerning a collective agreement that has been concluded, its result will be valid irrespective of the participation rate. If a collective agreement applies to only part of the union members or employees of an enterprise, it may be stipulated in the agreement that these persons only shall have the right to vote concerning it, provided it is stated clearly how the ballot is to be held (Article 5:3 of the TUI Act).

## III. Types of Collective Agreement

*329.* There is in principle no legal distinction between different types of collective agreements in Iceland, which only mentions one particular type of collective agreement – workplace agreements. However, since the enactment of the TUI Act some different forms of collective agreements have developed, the most common form being general collective agreements (*almennir kjarasamningar/heildarkjarasamningar*). ·

### A. General Collective Agreements

*330.* General collective agreements are usually negotiated by the national confederations, in most cases ASÍ and SA, on behalf of several or all of their member unions. Each of the national federations/unions then negotiates at least one general collective agreement which applies to wages and other terms of employment for all their members. These general agreements contain all relevant provisions, such as pay, working time, meal and coffee breaks, payments in cases of sickness and work-related accidents, holidays and holiday payments, health and safety at the workplace, payment of union fees, choice and duties of trade union representatives. General collective agreements are in several occupational sectors supplemented with so-called special agreements (*sérkjarasamningar*). General collective agreements are put up for vote among the union members the agreement applies to, unless the negotiating committee decides otherwise (cf. the TUI Act).

### B. Special Agreements

*331.* Special agreements are negotiated by one or more trade union at the local level with one or more companies in the same occupation, like the aluminium plants, where special conditions and working arrangements are taken into account. These special agreements, which in particular have been relevant for shift work, are normally considered a part of the relevant general agreement and usually have the same duration. These types of agreement usually only cover specific aspects and refer to general collective agreements on all other matters. In recent years the number of special agreements has decreased and their terms have been included in supplements to general collective agreements, commonly referred to as 'company-related parts of collective agreements', which are discussed below.

*332.* Special agreements are put to the vote among employees in the relevant companies or conglomerate.

### C. Workplace Agreements

*333.* Workplace agreements (*vinnustaðasamningar*) have since 1996 been defined in the TUI Act as collective agreements for trade union members at the same place of work where two or more unions are involved. This type of collective agreement has been negotiated for large industrial companies such as aluminium corporations and hydroelectric power plant projects. In those cases agreements can be negotiated on behalf of a number of trade unions belonging to different occupational sectors and national federations. Such agreements cover all the relevant issues that a general collective agreement would cover. These agreements have autonomy in relation to other agreements, both in terms of content and expiry date. This arrangement allows enterprises to negotiate with all their employees at their same time which can have considerable advantages over negotiating numerous agreements with different unions and different duration times.

*334.* Workplace agreements are put to the vote among all employees at the relevant enterprise. However, those employees do not participate in voting on general collective agreements negotiated by their member unions.

### D. Enterprise Agreements

*335.* Enterprise agreements (*fyrirtækjasamningar*) are in general made between one national association of trade unions and a particular company. This type of collective agreement can cover one or more member unions within the national association. Enterprise agreements cannot either be independent or refer to the relevant collective agreement on certain matters. When an enterprise agreement is put to the vote, only members of the relevant trade unions participate.

### E. Company-Related Parts of Collective Agreements

*336.* Since 1997 all general collective agreements have contained a chapter called company-related parts of collective agreements (*fyrirtækjadáttur kjarasamninga*). These company-related parts concern the alignment of the collective agreement to the requirements of the workplace and enhance the cooperation of employees and management at the workplace. The representatives of the employers and the employees thus get permission to negotiate in more detail on various provisions in the general collective agreement and conclude a section for that purpose which is then integrated into the relevant collective agreement. Both parties can propose negotiation regarding a company-related part to a collective agreement. Shop stewards usually represent employees in such negotiations with employers. Such company-related parts of collective agreements cover various issues such as flexible daytime work, shift work, production-related payment system. The provisions of the relevant collective agreement are fully in force regarding those aspects not covered specifically in the company-related part, which cannot include provisions that contradict or diminish the rights provided in the applicable collective agreement. However, a company-related part of a collective agreement can include authorization to adapt certain provisions in the collective agreement to fit the need of the company in question, regarding specific components. In such cases, the relevant trade union must make sure that the agreed variation and related compensation meet the legal provisions and collective agreements on minimum wages. It should furthermore be mentioned that this type of agreement does not in itself constitute a collective agreement unless a union is a party to it. However, relevant unions can nevertheless be called upon to participate as advisors.

*337.* The scope of a company-related part of a collective agreement can extend to all employees in the relevant company, individual groups or professions or even just individual departments.

*338.* The company-related part is put up for a vote among those employees covered by the agreement.

## IV. Content of Collective Agreements

*339.* Though the TUI Act has a number of provisions concerning collective agreements it is silent as to their content. Their content and coverage can be very different from one time to another. Among the factors influencing the coverage of collective agreements from time to time is the interaction of the common will of the social partners and how the government assesses its own position and strength. Usually collective agreements almost exclusively cover wages and terms of work, but there have also been agreements dealing with economic policy and industrial affairs (cf. in particular the 1990 National Social Pacts (*thjódarsáttarsamningarnir*)).

*340.* The content of collective agreement in Iceland can in general be divided into three main categories. The first category involves rates of pay depending on various factors, divided into daytime and overtime rates, and the influence of other factors such as type of work, age and work experience. The second relates to other individual rights than wages, such as holiday payments, working hours, minimum daily and weekly rest, shift work, workers' health and safety in the workplace, meal and coffee breaks, payments in cases of illness and work-related accidents, arrangement of working clothes, payment of union fees, choice and duties of trade union representatives. The third part concerns term of the agreement and in some cases dispute resolution of the negotiating parties and impact of changes in the underlying economic factors such as price increases, inflation levels which can influence the expected outcome of real wages during the time of validity of the agreement and its period of validity. The priority clauses (*see* paragraphs 251, 252) can be classified in this group of provisions since their purpose is to strengthen the trade unions as social units.

## V. Industrial Peace

*341.* When a collective agreement has been signed, the negotiating parties waive their right to take collective action inasmuch as the conditions established in the collective agreement are fully respected. Thus, a period of industrial peace is in principle to prevail for the validity of each collective agreement. Disputes regarding interpretation of collective agreements are to be referred to the Labour Court (*see* further in paragraph 351).

## VI. Extension and Coverage of Collective Agreements

*342.* As stated above the provisions of collective agreements are considered to be minimum working terms on the labour market and it is not a condition for applicability of a collective agreement that employees are members of the signatory trade union or that the employer in question is a member of the negotiating partner or the employers federation.

*343.* The extension and coverage of a collective agreement are in general seen as twofold. First, in accordance with the 1980 WTP Act, the occupational coverage of a collective agreement is linked to the mandated occupational area of the signatory trade union and covers all work that is customarily performed by employees who are members of the signatory union or is performed by workers engaged in the same type of work that the agreement applies to. Second, the geographical coverage depends on the material scope of the agreement on the one hand and the limits posed on by the geographical district of the negotiating trade union on the other.

*344.* A collective agreement is binding for a member of trade union even though he resigns from the union and is no longer a member of it, while he continues to engage in the type of work covered by the agreement concerned until the agreement could at the earliest be invalidated in accordance with notice of termination (Article 3:2 of the TUI Act).

## VII. Negotiating Schedule

*345.* In 1996 the TUI Act was amended to include among other things provisions on a negotiating schedule; previously the parties of a collective agreement did not have a legal right to enter into discussion with the respondent. Employers, or their organizations, and trade unions, have to draw up a schedule for the conduct of negotiations on the renewal of collective agreements. The contracting parties may grant their national or overall federations a special mandate to draw up negotiation schedules on their behalf if such a mandate is not provided for in the lawful constitutions of the contracting parties' federations or organizations. Negotiation schedules, signed by both contracting parties, shall be sent to the SCMO immediately.

*346.* A negotiating schedule shall be drawn up not later than ten weeks before the valid collective agreement comes up for review. If the contracting parties have not made a negotiating schedule by this date, the conciliation and mediation officer shall issue a negotiating schedule for the contracting parties not later than eight weeks before the valid collective agreement comes up for review, in which case the conciliation and mediation officer shall take account of other negotiating schedules that have been made (Article 23 of the TUI Act).

## VIII. Duration and Termination of Collective Agreements

*347.* Collective agreements are concluded for a specific period of time. If the parties have not concluded a new agreement before the old one expires, the terms of the old agreement will apply until a new agreement has been signed. Collective agreements have in recent years been concluded for a period of three to four years. The period of validity of special agreements made to supplement general collective agreements is usually linked to the validity of the general collective agreement which it adheres to.

*348.* In general, collective agreements contain provisions concerning termination and usually they stipulate that the agreement is valid for a certain period and will expire on a certain date without termination. Notice of termination of an agreement shall be in writing. If a collective agreement does not include provision on duration and/or termination, the period of validity shall be one year and respite for notice of termination shall be three months (Article 6 of the TUI Act).

*349.* Collective agreements sometimes contain provisions stipulating that they may be partly terminated. If there are no such provisions, the agreement will not be terminated except in its entirety. As a customary rule, a collective agreement will still apply in the relations of the parties until a new collective agreement has been agreed upon or a strike begins.

*350.* Collective agreements can furthermore be annulled under the general rules of contract law, but there would have to be substantial reasons for such action.

## IX. Interpretation of Collective Agreements

*351.* The interpretation of collective agreements is subject to similar rules like other contracts, under the general rules of contract law, taking into account the particularities of such agreements. Collective agreements often include provisions stipulating that differences which come up in the duration of the agreement shall be dealt with by a joint committee of the contracting partners. This is particularly common in the public sector. If there is no such provision or if a joint committee of the parties does not bring the dispute to a conclusion, it may be referred to the Labour Court.

§3. The Public Sector

*352.* Public servants in Iceland did not enjoy the right to bargain collectively until 1962. Prior to that, decisions concerning their wages and terms were taken unilaterally by the legislator, for civil servants, and local government, for local government employees. This was amended by legislation in 1962, when public servants were granted limited negotiating rights.

*353.* Under the existing legislation on the collective agreement of public servants, the 1986 CAPS Act, trade unions and their federations have to meet certain criteria in order to obtain the right to bargain collectively. The confederations which now fulfil these criteria are trade unions within BHM, KÍ and BSRB, in addition to a few trade unions which operate outside the federations. The CAPS Act also lays down that only one trade union shall have the right to negotiate agreements with the same employer for the same class of employees. The trade unions are the proper legal contracting partners to negotiate and conclude collective agreements for their members but can delegate the right of making agreements to their confederations. In addition the Act contains provisions concerning the content of collective agreements, their duration and accountability. A collective agreement in the public sector shall specify wages, working hours, overtime rates, holidays, travel costs, eating facilities and food prices, insurance, staff training and other matters upon which the parties come to agreement. The agreements shall be in writing and shall stipulate the duration and notice of termination (Articles 9–10 of the CAPS Act). If a collective agreement is terminated it should nevertheless be followed until a new collective agreement comes into force (Article 12).

*354.* The board of the Association of Local Authorities in Iceland (*Stjórn Sambands íslenskra sveitarfélaga*) has since 2010 been the representative body, but the city of Reykjavík negotiates separately. Icelandic local authorities operate on the basis of the 2011 Local Government Act, according to which their employees' salaries, rights and obligations shall be subject to collective agreements in force at any time and/or the terms of the contract of employment. As described below (paragraph 355) there has been some decentralization of collective bargaining for state employees, but at the municipality level the wage negotiating process still remains centralized.

*355.* In 1997 significant changes were made to the wage structure for state employees, which had been very rigid before that time. The changes resulted in decentralization of the wage negotiation process as the negotiations were split in two. First, there is a central contract between the union and the Ministry of Finance, where so-called frameworks are defined. In the second stage of negotiation, the members of a specific union in each workplace negotiate with the head of each institute on how the contract will be applied to that particular workplace, based on the broad definition given in the central agreement. Thus, an additional agreement, the institutional agreement, is made within each institute with each union operating in that institute. This institutional agreement is considered a part of the collective bargaining agreement.

# Chapter 5. Strikes, Lockouts and Other Legal Forms of Industrial Action

§1. DIFFERENT CATEGORIES OF COLLECTIVE INDUSTRIAL ACTION

*356.* The TUI Act recognizes the right of trade unions, employers' associations and individual employers to declare a work stoppage for the purpose of working for the advancement of their demands in industrial disputes and for the protection of their rights under the Act, subject only to the conditions and limitations which are laid down in laws. The term 'work stoppage' refers to lockouts by employers and strikes in which workers discontinue their normal work to some extent or in its entirety in order to achieve a specific common goal. The term also applies to other comparable actions taken by employers or workers, which may be regarded as the equivalent of work stoppages. Such actions can include the refusal to work over-time, on weekends or perform certain aspects of the work in question as well as slowing down work from what is considered normal working speed. If such actions qualify as a comparable measure to strike or lockout, it may be considered a legal work stoppage, but the legislation makes no distinction between the different forms. In addition to the TUI Act, the CAPS Act applies to the public sector.

## I. Strike

*357.* The definition of a strike entails that a group of employees with a common purpose stop work or refuse to begin work, in order to enforce their demands. In fact, strikes are used as a bargaining tool by trade unions when negotiating a new collective agreement.

*358.* Generally, the execution of strikes in Iceland involves everyone who performs tasks covered by the relevant collective agreement stopping work completely. The extension of the strike is, however, under the control of the relevant trade union and can cover the union members as a whole, a particular profession or a particular workplace. Although the most common form of strike includes total work stoppage, there have been cases of limited actions such as refusals to perform certain aspects of the work, refusal to work overtime and weekends as well as gradual reduction in performance. Such collective actions have been considered to meet the definition of a strike by the Icelandic Labour Court. Furthermore, it has been considered to constitute a strike when a group of employees terminate their employment contracts in order to enforce their demands.

*359.* Individual employees or groups of employees without union membership do not have the right to call a strike under the TUI Act, and a decision on their behalf to shut down work will therefore not be considered a strike within the meaning of the Act.

## II.  Lockouts

*360.*  The concept of lockouts is not explicitly defined in the TUI Act but has been defined through case law and by Icelandic scholars as covering situations when one or more employers prohibit work, in part or in whole, by workers who are members of one or more trade unions for the purpose of promoting their claims in industrial disputes and/or protect their rights under the TUI Act. Some scholars have defined the term as work stoppage which entails one or more employers terminating the employment relationships of a group of employees or refusing to receive the services of a group of employees, without the dismissal or refusal being caused by operational considerations. This second definition has not achieved broad consensus, since the definition of termination of employment is generally used in situations when the employment relationship is intended to come to an end on a permanent basis. Lockouts, however, are actions that employers can utilize during industrial disputes and are mainly used as a counteraction in cases of strikes by trade union members in Iceland.

*361.*  The TUI Act is mainly drafted with regard to strikes, but since the provisions are intended to apply to all forms of work stoppage they cover lockouts as well. Strikes are, however, much more frequent than lockouts, which are rarely applied in Iceland. Nevertheless, the fundamental rule when it comes to work stoppage is the principle of reciprocity; hence, the same requirements and the same rules apply whether a trade union initiates a strike or an employer calls a lockout.

*362.*  It is clearly stated in both the TUI Act and case law that employers have the right to use lockouts for the purpose of working for the advancement of their demands or the protection of their rights under law in industrial disputes. Employers cannot, however, utilize this measure in order to conserve costs or in cases where there is a lack of projects.

## III.  Sympathy Action

*363.*  The legitimacy of sympathy actions derives from interpretation of the TUI Act (Article 17) as well as Labour Court case law and is commonly recognized if the actions support a legitimate strike. Sympathy action differs from the traditional definition of a strike; thus, the aim is promoting the claims of a different group than the one who actually performs the sympathy action. In order for an industrial action to be classified as a sympathy action, the participants cannot include their own demands but only require that the demands of others are met. If the purpose was to promote or enforce their own demands, the action would be considered to constitute a strike in the traditional meaning of the term. Hence, the definition of a sympathy action is based on the purpose and support function the action is founded on.

*364.*  Since sympathy actions have the purpose of supporting the demands of others, the peace obligation (*see* further paragraphs 365–367) does not prevent such measures being taken when a valid collective agreement is in place. Furthermore, the Labour Court has determined that it can be legitimate to enforce sympathy actions in Iceland to support a legitimate strike abroad.

## §2. LEGITIMACY OF WORK STOPPAGES

### I. The Peace Obligation

*365.* The peace obligation is a fundamental rule in Icelandic labour law. The rule entails the conclusion that a collective agreement has the effect of making collective industrial action illegal during the validity of the agreement. Hence, actions or attempts to gain improvements on the stipulations of the existing agreement must be considered contrary to the postulation and prerequisites of that agreement.

*366.* The right to strike does therefore not exist if there is a valid agreement between a trade union and employers regarding workers' wages and terms. It is thus not allowed to commence a work stoppage due to a disagreement concerning a collective agreement, its understanding or value. That kind of disagreement must be brought before the Labour Court. Consequently, the peace obligation has the effect that a work stoppage can only be commenced when collective agreements are open for review or if there has been no collective agreement between the parties concerned. This applies not only to strikes and lockouts but also all other comparable measures taken by employers or employees which may be regarded as the equivalent of work stoppages.

*367.* There are only two exemptions to the peace obligation rule under the TUI Act. First, notwithstanding the rule, it is permissible to commence stoppage of work for the enforcement of a Labour Court decree. Second, such action can be taken in support of a union having commenced lawful stoppage of work, e.g., sympathy action, whether a collective agreement is in force or not. Besides this, single employees or groups of employees may be entitled to shut down work under certain circumstances without breaking the peace obligation rule. This mainly applies in situations when the health and safety at the working place are significantly deficient but can also pertain if employees are subjected to physical violence or the threat of physical violence by the employer. Discontent and/or conflict in the workplace due to management, has, however, not been considered to constitute a lawful foundation for work stoppage. In principle, all exceptions to the peace obligation are interpreted narrowly by Icelandic courts.

### II. Unlawful Work Stoppages

*368.* As described earlier (*see* paragraphs 365–367) the peace obligation is a fundamental rule in the Icelandic labour market; hence, all work stoppages occurring while valid collective agreements are in force are unlawful, except under very specific circumstances covered in paragraph 367.

121

*369.* As stated above, employers' associations and individual employers are authorized to declare strikes and lockouts for the purpose of working for the advancement of their demands in industrial disputes and for the protection of their rights. Demands made by either party must be lawful in nature, and the purpose of industrial action must be to achieve collective demands and will otherwise be deemed unlawful; this would for example be the case if an employer conducted a lockout to save the cost of paying wages when there was a lack of projects.

*370.* It is not permissible to commence stoppage of work in cases of disputes that only concern issues that fall under the jurisdiction of the Labour Court, except for the enforcement of the Court's decree (Article 17 of the TUI Act). Issues such as the interpretation or violation of collective agreements or employment contracts fall under the scope of the Labour Court and cannot therefore be the basis for work stoppage. It is not permissible accordingly to commence stoppage of work in cases where the purpose of the action is to force the authorities to perform acts which they are not duty-bound to undertake or not to perform acts which they must undertake according to laws provided that these are not acts to which the authorities are a party in the capacity of employers. Additionally the article forbids work stoppage in support of a union that has commenced an unlawful stoppage of work.

## III. Work Stoppage Monitoring

*371.* When a legitimate work stoppage is in progress, unions traditionally monitor whether it is being respected. Representatives of the participating union go between posts and make sure that the positions of their members are not being filled by other employees and that those working have the authority to do so. The authorization for such monitoring is based on the TUI Act (Article 18), which stipulates that when a work stoppage has been commenced in a lawful manner, those against whom it is in some respect directed are not permitted to promote the prevention thereof with the assistance of individual members of the unions or federations being parties to the stoppage of work. Certain procedures have been formed regarding this monitoring, and any requests for exemptions are addressed to the relevant union. When monitoring whether the rules and procedures of a work stoppage are being followed, the monitors are bound by the scope of Article 18 and cannot participate in actions that fall under the authority of law enforcement. It is not uncommon for the monitoring to cause considerable controversy and clashes between the disputing parties, which can in some cases lead to violence. Law enforcement is banned from intervening in industrial actions in other ways than to keep the peace and prevent violence and injury. The involvement of law enforcement during industrial disputes is almost invariably associated with conflicts deriving from work stoppage monitoring. Although Icelandic law is considered to grant unions the authority to have their representatives monitor work stoppages, the resolution on whether they go beyond the scope of that authority is subject to the decree of the judicial system. According to case law, unions can become liable and made to pay both compensation and punitive damages if their actions in relation to work stoppage monitoring go beyond the scope of the TUI Act.

§3. FORMAL REQUIREMENTS OF NOTICE

*372.* The formal rules and requirements regarding work stoppage are stipulated in the TUI Act. The rules pertaining to decisions on declaring work stoppages are compulsory, and the Labour Court has put emphasis on their being followed to the utmost extent, otherwise deeming the action unlawful. A work stoppage can only be decided on by a general secret ballot with the participation of at least one-fifth of the members with a right to vote according to the voting roll or members' register, and if the proposal has received the support of the majority of the votes cast (Article 15a). A general secret postal ballot may be held among the members concerning a proposal for a work stoppage, and its result will be valid irrespective of the participation rate. If a work stoppage is intended to involve only a particular group of union members or employees at a specified working place, a decision concerning the work stoppage may be taken on the basis of the votes of those whom it is intended to involve. In such a case, one-fifth of those with the right to vote must take part in the ballot, and the majority of them must support the proposal for a work stoppage. A proposal for a work stoppage should state clearly to whom it is specifically intended to apply and when it is planned to implement the stoppage. For a decision to call a work stoppage to be legal, negotiations or attempts at negotiations on the demands presented must have proved fruitless despite the efforts of a conciliation and mediation officer. It is thus a legal requirement that convening negotiations or consultation efforts on the submitted demands have been exhausted before a work stoppage is called. There are, however, no rules or standards regarding the assessment on when the negotiations or consultations have proved fruitless. The assessment is therefore made by the party who ends the negotiation and seeks permission to declare a work stoppage, usually with a statement or declaration directed to both the other party as well as the conciliator. Nevertheless, a negotiating committee or the competent representatives of the contracting parties may at all times cancel a work stoppage after it has been declared. The same parties may postpone a work stoppage that has been called, once or more often, by up to twenty-eight days in total, without the approval of the opposite contracting party, providing that party is informed of the postponement with at least three days' notice.

*373.* A decision on a work stoppage, for the purpose of enforcing an amendment to or decision upon wages and terms, should be made known to the conciliation and mediation officer and those against whom such action is mainly directed, seven days prior to the intended commencement of such action. The notice of work stoppage must have reached those whom it is directed to seven days before the intended work stoppage is to begin. The notice is considered having reached the recipients when they have truly had the opportunity to access the message, for example a letter placed in a mailbox or a notification letter has been delivered. The party giving the notice bears the burden of proof that the notice has reached the receivers in accordance with TUI Act. Any deviation from the rules of notification results in the unlawfulness of the intended collective actions.

## I. Form and Content of the Notice

*374.* The TUI Act does not address the form of the notice. The importance of being able to prove that the notice has reached the intended recipients, within a specified timeframe, results in the notification always being put forward in writing. Conventionally the notice is delivered in the form of a letter where the recipient signs for the delivery.

*375.* It is an accepted practice in Iceland that a work stoppage notification is clearly worded leaving no room for questions regarding when or how the work stoppage is to be carried out. Generally, the intended date and time are noted but if there is no specific time specified the Labour Court has ruled that the work stoppage comes into effect at midnight on the date in question. The notice has to include all relevant information regarding the work stoppage, including when it is to begin and how it is to be performed. Information regarding who declares a work stoppage and whom it is directed to must be clearly stated as well as how the decision for the action was taken. If the work stoppage only reaches certain employees, tasks or workplaces it should be made known in the notice.

## II. Competence to Give Notice

*376.* Trade unions, employers' associations and single employers have the competence to declare a work stoppage (Article 14 of the TUI Act). On the other, confederations of trade unions and confederations of employers do in general not have the competence to give notice; hence, it is the responsibility of the individual member unions or associations to give notice on the behalf of their members, even in cases of concerted actions. However, SA is authorized by its statutes to give notice on the behalf of its members, provided that the employers in question have a direct membership of the confederation. Individual employees or groups of employees without union membership do not, however, possess this right under the TUI Act, and a decision on their behalf to shut down work would therefore not fall within its scope.

§4. Consequences of Such Actions

*377.* The employment relationship continues during work stoppages, but the main duties of the employment relationship are inactive during the action; hence, wages are not paid and employees do not have to perform any of their duties deriving from the employment contract. Employees are not entitled to sick pay during work stoppage either due to illness or work accidents, even though the sick leave had started when the work stoppage was commenced. If employees are on vacation during a work stoppage, the duration of the work stoppage will not be deducted from the employees' vacation days.

*378.* At the conclusion of a work stoppage the employment relationship continues unchanged and the duties of both parties come in effect. Consequently, employees are obliged to return to work and employers are obliged to accept their work contribution. Since work stoppages are socially motivated actions primarily under the control of trade unions and employers' associations, they do not have an effect on the individual employment relationship between employees and employers. This is, however, not without exceptions, since examples can be found of collective agreements including provisions which allow employees to terminate the employment contract during or following a work stoppage without a notice period. Employers on the other must respect the notice period, if they intend to terminate the employment relationship following a work stoppage. It should, however, be noted that the TUI Act forbids employers to attempt to influence their employer attitudes in dealings with trade unions or in relation to industrial disputes by notice of termination of employment or threats of such notice (Article 4).

## I. Accumulation of Rights

*379.* When it comes to the accumulation of rights during stoppage of work it is general practice in the Icelandic labour market that the time lost due to such actions is regarded as working time when employees' rights are calculated.

*380.* The 1979 Act on Respecting Labourers' Right to Advance Notice of Termination of Employment, etc. (TEIA Act, 19/1979) determines the minimum rules regarding accumulation of rights regarding notice of termination and sick leave. Employees are considered to have worked within a trade or to have been engaged with an employer for one year if they have served a total of at the least 1550 hours during the last 12 months, thereof at the least 130 hours during the last month prior to notice of termination (Article 1). In this connection absence on account of illness, accidents, vacation, strikes and lockouts of up to eight hours per day is considered the equivalent of hours of work discharged. According to this, time lost from work due to work stoppage does not affect the assessment of working length and the accumulation of rights based thereon.

*381.* The 1987 Holiday Allowance Act does not specifically address the impact of work stoppage on holiday rights. The Act specifies that absence on the grounds of illness, injury or vacation does not affect an employee's right to holiday and the accumulation of holiday time, and although it is not specifically mentioned it has been generally accepted that work stoppages do not affect the accumulation of holiday entitlements either (Article 3). This is based on the principal rule of the Holiday Allowance Act that all employees have the minimum entitlement to leave under the Act. However, work stoppage affects the accumulation of holiday pay which is calculated as a proportion of the employee's wages within the holiday period and time periods without wages are reduced proportionally.

*382.* When it comes to seniority provisions, these are based on the date the employee started work and it is generally assumed that work stoppage has no influence regarding this matter. It is also a factor in this regard that industrial actions usually last for a short time, measured in days or weeks, but seniority provisions are based on a longer period, customarily considered in years.

## II. Work During Work Stoppage

*383.* As previously stated, the purpose of collective industrial actions is to achieve certain demands and it is therefore in the nature of work stoppages to cease work. The TUI Act stipulates that when a stoppage of work has been commenced in a lawful manner it is not permitted to promote the preventions thereof with the assistance of individual members of the unions or federations being parties to the work stoppage. An employee is therefore not permitted to perform his own work duties or the duties of others who are party to a work stoppage; hence, it is not permitted to perform duties that fall under the scope of the relevant collective agreement during collective industrial actions (Article 18).

*384.* This raises the question of whether employees can take on other jobs during a work stoppage. The TUI Act does not address this issue directly, but the statutes of the Confederation of Employers (SA) include a provision that forbids members to hire employees participating in a work stoppage involving another member employer. The commission of SA can furthermore decide that the stipulation includes work stoppages abroad.

*385.* Restrictions regarding work during work stoppage are therefore primarily found in the SA statutes. However, employees can seek work outside the SA members without any restrictions, provided the work in question is not covered by a collective agreement which is the basis for an ongoing industrial action. Nevertheless, SA statutes also include a provision allowing them to boycott non-member employers in cases where they are presumed to work directly against the interests of members involved in an industrial dispute, for example by hiring employees during a work stoppage.

## III. Liability

*386.* According to the TUI Act trade unions are responsible for any breach of agreement which the union itself or its lawfully appointed shop stewards commit in connection with their functions of trust for the union (Article 8). The trade union will be held responsible for breaches of agreements by its individual member only provided the union will be blamed for the breach of agreement. The Labour Court has several times determined that a union was responsible for unlawful industrial actions and therefore liable.

*387.* Individual employees can also bear responsibility when it comes to unlawful industrial actions and become liable under the general rules of tort for damages they cause. In these cases it is not a factor whether or not the relevant union bears joint responsibility or whether the individual employee in question acted without the unions consent or knowledge. Generally, however, legal measures are only taken against the trade union involved and not individual employees, although some examples are to the contrary.

*388.* Furthermore, according to the TUI Act, non-federated employers and non-unionized employees are solely responsible for breaches of agreement which they cause (Article 8:2). If it is not demonstrated that a contracting party has taken part in measures which may be regarded as work stoppages, each union member shall be responsible for his participation in such measures.

*389.* Industrial actions on the behalf of employers do not fall under the scope of previously mentioned provisions of the TUI Act. Nevertheless, employers can be deemed liable in cases of illegal lockouts, primarily with the payment of compensation for loss of income for the duration of the lockout.

*390.* On the basis of the TUI Act, the Labour Court can order parties to pay damages, fines and costs in accordance with customary rules (Article 65). In determining the amount of damages regard may be had for the culpability of the violation. In principal, the general rules of tort apply when it comes to the determination of damages due to unlawful industrial action. Compensation is based on the 'culpa rule' under which a person is liable for damages, if the action leading to the damage is caused with criminal or illegal means, provided that the damage is a probable consequence of the action in question.

## IV. Government Intervention

*391.* The Supreme Court has deemed that the right to strike is protected under the Constitution and that this right may only be restricted under the conditions stipulated in Article 11, paragraph 2 of the ECHR. Hence, no restrictions can be placed on the exercise of these rights other than those prescribed by law and are necessary in a democratic society in the interest of national security or public safety. The article does not, however, prevent authorities from imposing lawful restrictions regarding the exercise of these rights by members of the police or of the administration of the state.

*392.* There is no general system of arbitration to terminate a work stoppage under the TUI Act, and it is not common for the parties to agree upon such a solution. The basic principle has been that industrial disputes should be resolved by means of negotiation and bargaining. There is furthermore a strong demand that a work stoppage is only utilized when the negotiating parties have exhausted all attempts to reach an agreement. For this reason, the TUI Act was amended in 1996

to stipulate that for a work stoppage to be legal, negotiations or attempts at negotiations on the demands presented must have proved fruitless despite the efforts of
a conciliation and mediation officer.

*393.* Work stoppages were quite common in Iceland before the 1990 National
Social Pact (*Thjóðarsáttarsamningarnir*), but their frequency has declined considerably since then. In the Icelandic labour market, the potency of relatively small
unions or groups of comparatively well-paid employees in key positions, for
example flight operations, has proved to be problematic on account of the broad
impact industrial action on their behalf has on the community. Government intervention regarding work stoppages is most commonly directed at these groups,
although there are examples of such actions being utilized with regard to other
trades.

*394.* During the years 1985–2010 the Icelandic government intervened in industrial action on twelve occasions, with legislation passed by Althingi: three times
concerning flight operations, once concerning dairy scientists, five concerning fishermen, two concerning public employees and once to prohibit work stoppages in
general. Government intervention with legislation banning work stoppages is without exception enforced on the grounds of economic justifications or that impending
action will negatively affect public interests.

*395.* The authorities can intervene in industrial disputes with legislation at any
point in time, provided there are sufficient grounds for such actions. Hence, ranging
from before work stoppage begins and until it has been ongoing for such a long time
that there is no outlook for achieving reconciliation, legislation can be utilized to
cease industrial actions. Legislation ceasing industrial actions usually establishes an
arbitration panel, typically composed of three members of the Supreme Court, who
are to decide on wages and other terms of the disputing parties. The arbitration panel
is then guided to take into account the wage development of similar professions or
groups of employees as well as collective development in the society.

*396.* The legitimacy of actions on the behalf of the legislator putting a stop to
industrial action and thereby limiting constitutional rights is subject to the decree of
the Supreme Court. The constitutional value of such legislation has, however, on
only one occasion been the subject of the Court decree. This was in the case of the
2001 Act on the Pay and Conditions of Fishermen (34/2001) (cf. Supreme Court
Case No. 167/2002), where the Court was persuaded that the economic justifications and the public interest in putting a stop to the ongoing work stoppage had been
adequate and sufficient grounds for the government intervention at that time. Furthermore, the Court determined that the legislator had not gone further than necessary in limiting constitutional rights in order to achieve the goal of ensuring the
common good. ASÍ did also address a complaint to the ILO Freedom of Association Committee regarding the government intervention which came to a result contrary to the aforementioned Supreme Court verdict. The Committee concluded that
the legislation included various terms involving violations of ILO Conventions

nos. 87 (1948) and 98 (1949) and that the economic assumptions which were the foundation of the legislation were not sufficient justification for such restrictions on the right to impose industrial action.

## §5. THE PUBLIC SECTOR

*397.* For a long time public sector employees were forbidden to participate in industrial action, under the 1915 Act on Public Sector Strikes (33/1915). It was not until 1976 that public sector employees who were members of BSRB were granted the right to strike in order to compel the conclusion of collective agreements. This right was, however, limited in several ways, and the prelude to such actions was quite different than on the private labour market. Other associations of public sector employees were not granted these rights until 1986, and still today the Act from 1915 applies to certain groups of public employees, who are not allowed to strike.

*398.* As in the private sector, public employees are authorized to utilize industrial actions for the purpose of working for the advancement of their demands in industrial disputes and for the protection of their rights. The CAPS Act from 1986 does, however, place certain restrictions on the public sector in relations to industrial actions. Hence, only unions in the public sector have the right to commence work stoppage, but employers, i.e., the government and local authorities, do not have such a right. The Act demands greater participation of members to decide on commencing a work stoppage than in the private sector. The decision has to be taken by secret ballot and requires at least half of the members to participate in the vote and the majority of them to endorse the proposal. Additionally, the notice of intended industrial actions in the public sector is fifteen days compared to seven days in the private sector.

*399.* Certain groups of public employees are not allowed to participate in industrial actions under Article 19 of the CAPS Act. Those are:

(1) all officials and in addition other Government employees covered by the State Salaries Commission;
(2) employees of Parliament and its institutions as well as employees at the office of the President of Iceland and employees of the Government Office, including employees of the Foreign Service;
(3) all employees of the Supreme Court, the Court of Appeal and District Courts;
(4) employees in the office of Public Prosecutions and the State Attorney's office;
(5) employees who work with security and basic health services;
(6) managers, clerks, engineers, office managers and staff payroll division of local, city and municipal authorities;
(7) heads of major business and local service organizations;
(8) employees whose work is compatible with those mentioned in points 6 and 7.

*400.* According to the second paragraph of Article 19, the Finance Minister and local authorities, following consultation with the relevant trade unions, are to publish a report with information entailing the work which is covered by points (5–8) of the article, before the first of February each year. Controversies and objections to the report are subject to the decision of the Labour Court.

*401.* Additionally, the provision of Article 20 of the CAPS Act authorizes authorities to call employees who are participating in a legal work stoppage back to work temporarily in order to prevent crises. However, authorities cannot exercise this authority by their own preferences. A committee of two men, one nominated by the relevant union and the other by the appropriate Government or local authority, decides who should be summoned back to work under the article. It is furthermore required that both committee members agree on a decision regarding recall to work (Article 21). The decision is final and is not subject to appeal to either the Labour Court or other higher authorities.

*402.* In other ways than has been described, the provisions of the CAPS Act are comparable with the TUI Act in regard to work stoppage and employees' rights thereof. In order to make the status of those public employees who are members of unions operating on the private market more compatible to other public employees, it was negotiated in collective agreements that these groups fall under the scope of the CAPS Act in regard to work stoppage. However, following the privatization of government assets, a considerable number of employees who formerly belonged to the public sector are now considered to be employees in the private sector and therefore fall under the TUI Act.

## §6. STATISTICS

*403.* Prior to the adoption of the TUI Act in 1938, industrial actions were frequent and particularly aimed at getting employers to recognize unions and their right to collectively bargain on the behalf of their members as well as resisting wage reductions. The main objective of the TUI Act was to ensure peace and stability on the labour market and to minimize impairment to the labour market in cases of industrial dispute. Despite the existence of the legislation, work stoppages were quite common in the private sector in the years following its adoption. This has been partly attributed to the former arrangement of collective bargaining and instability of the economic environment. However, in recent decades the frequency of work stoppages has declined considerably. This has among other factors been attributed to the nationwide collective agreements concluded in 1986 (*Thjóðarsáttarsamningarnir fyrri*), and the National Social Pacts from 1990, which were collaborative efforts made by the social partners and the government to combat inflation and ensure stability. This created a favourable economic climate in which real wages rose and inflation remained low. The National Social Pacts were based on mutual trust between the social parties and government officials, and subsequent collective agreements were concluded for longer periods than had been customary before, or up to four years. In addition, the collective bargaining process

changed in 1996 when the TUI Act was amended, providing rules regarding negotiation and mediation efforts as well as specific rules of notice as a precursor to
industrial actions. Prior to the amendment it was common for the negotiating parties to decide upon actions in small meetings and without the majority vote of members, communications between the social parties were in many cases lacking and the
negotiation process and strategy insufficient. There has been a dramatic decline in
industrial action since the beginning of the 1980s, and in the last few years such
actions have reached an all-time minimum.

404. As previously covered in paragraph 397, public sector employees did not
enjoy the right to utilize industrial action until 1976. Following the extension of
these rights there were a considerable number of strikes in the public sector. While
the rate of industrial actions has in general been declining in Iceland in the last
decades, it has increased among public employees, especially in the education and
care sectors.

# Chapter 6. Settlement of Industrial Disputes and Protection of Vital Needs

## §1. INDUSTRIAL DISPUTES

*405.* When it comes to industrial disputes in the Icelandic labour market, the TUI Act has in many ways institutionalized conflicts and formed a framework around the collective bargaining process where the peace obligation prevails. On this basis, communication on the labour market can be somewhat restrained although fully consistent with one of the main purpose of the TUI Act, to bring conflicts and disagreements under control by forming certain rules of procedures in order to prevent labour disputes resulting in damage to the economy and society.

*406.* As previously stated, when collective agreements are in force the peace obligation prevails and prevents all industrial action. Any disputes concerning the terms of existing collective agreements, whether they have been violated or regarding their interpretation, are considered to constitute a judicial dispute and are to be settled by the Labour Court. A judicial dispute cannot be the foundation for industrial action. Only disputes of interest can be the basis of such actions in the Icelandic labour market; hence, disputes regarding wages and terms arise at a time when collective agreements expire or no collective agreements are in force.

*407.* No later than ten weeks before a valid collective agreement comes up for review, employers, or their organizations, and trade unions must draw up a schedule for the conduct of negotiations on the renewal of collective agreements. The contracting parties may grant their national or overall federations a special mandate to draw up negotiation schedules on their behalf if such a mandate is not provided for in the lawful Constitutions of the contracting parities' federations or organizations. If negotiations between the contracting parties break down, or if either of them considers there is little hope of success being achieved through further attempts to reach a settlement, either of them or both, acting jointly, may refer the dispute to a conciliation and mediation officer. Furthermore, the contracting parties can at any time after the issue of a negotiation schedule request the assistance of a conciliation and mediation officer.

*408.* Where industrial disputes arise and the normal collective bargaining procedures do not prove adequate to resolve the conflict, the TUI Act stipulates that the State Conciliation and Meditation Officer is to handle facilitation of a settlement. It is generally presumed that under Icelandic labour law, authorities have no further role to play in disputes of interests than to facilitate settlements. However, the government is empowered to appoint a special conciliation committee if it appears proved that an industrial dispute will have extremely serious consequences as well as utilizing the legislation power to put an end to work stoppages under certain circumstances (*see* paragraphs 391–396).

§2. THE STATE CONCILIATION AND MEDITATION OFFICER

*409.* The function of conciliation and meditation was until 1978, carried out by a group of people who filled other positions, but in that year the role was made a full-time position of the State Conciliation and Meditation Officer (SCMO). The Minister of Social Affairs and Equality appoints a SCMO for the term of five years at a time. According to the TUI Act (Article 20), the SCMO must be an Icelandic citizen, in charge of his financial affairs and have an unblemished reputation. Furthermore, efforts must be made to ensure that his attitude is such that he may be regarded as impartial in matters involving employees and employers. As with the SCMO, the Minister of Welfare shall also appoint a Deputy SCMO, who shall fulfil the same requirements and take over the functions of the SCMO when he is indisposed as well as assisting him as the occasion demands. In addition, the SCMO can nominate Assistant SCMOs to assist him in the resolution of industrial disputes or to work independently at the resolution of an individual industrial dispute. It is considered to be a civic duty to undertake the work of an Assistant SCMO under the TUI Act. Both the Deputy State SCMO and Assistant SCMOs have the same rights and obligations as the SCMO when they are engaged in their work.

*410.* The SCMO shall work for conciliation in industrial disputes between employees and their unions, on the one hand, and employers and their associations on the other (Article 22 of the TUI Act). He shall monitor the situation and outlook in the economy and the employment market on a national level as well as keeping abreast of wages and terms situation and matters which may lead to disputes in relations between the parties on the labour market. The SCMO shall furthermore keep a register of valid collective agreements, and employees' and employers' organizations, and non-affiliated employers, are obliged to send him copies of all collective agreements they conclude as soon as they are signed. Amendments to previously made agreements shall be sent to him in the same way. The parties are furthermore obliged to turn over copies of all pay scales and terms of service issued on the basis of valid collective agreements as well as copies of terminations of wages and terms agreements, as soon as they are sent to their opposing parties.

§3. THE PROCESS OF CONCILIATION AND MEDITATION

*411.* When the SCMO receives a notification to the effect that negotiation between contracting parties prove fruitless or one or both of the contracting parties refer a dispute to him, he is obliged to call the contracting parties, or their representatives, to a meeting as soon as possible and to continue attempts at conciliation while there is hope that they will produce results. The SCMO shall take over the direction of the negotiations as proposed in the negotiation schedule put forward by the contracting parties (Article 24 of the TUI Act). He can, however, at any point in time postpone a formal attempt at conciliation and urge the contracting parties to try to explore possibilities for a settlement in direct negotiations between themselves if he considers that more likely to produce results as well as he can at any time take over the direction of negotiations if he considers that it would increase the possibility of results. If a work stoppage has been notified in accordance with the TUI Act (Article 16), the SCMO is obliged to work for conciliation between the disputing parties and direct their negotiations.

*412.* The contracting parties are obliged to attend, or have their representatives attend, any negotiation meeting to which they are called by a conciliation and mediation officer (Article 25 of the TUI Act). Conciliation meetings are always held behind closed doors, and at such meetings copies of the documents which have passed between the parties in the previous states of the dispute are presented, providing they have not already been sent to the SCMO. It is furthermore prohibited to publicize, or to take statements from witnesses concerning, discussions at conciliation meetings and proposals which may have been made, without the approval of both contracting parties. During such conciliation meetings, a conciliation and mediation officer may demand any reports and explanations which he considers necessary from the disputing parties as well as demanding such information and reports from all public bodies. All such items requested by a conciliation and mediation officer are to be treated with confidence, as stated in the TUI Act (Article 26).

*413.* When attempts to reach an agreement between the parties with conciliation prove fruitless, a conciliation and mediation officer submits a compromise proposal in the attempt to resolve the dispute and reach an agreement (*see* further in paragraph 416).

*414.* If those conciliation attempts by the conciliation and mediation officer end without result, they are to be resumed if either party so desires or the conciliation and mediation officer considers it appropriate. He shall at all times, however, attempt to achieve conciliation within fourteen days of having discontinued his previous attempts at conciliation (Article 35 of the TUI Act). Furthermore in cases when attempts at conciliation in an important dispute are discontinued without result, the SCMO may publish a report in the matter in the manner he considers best designed to give the public a true picture of the dispute.

*415.* A conciliation and mediation officer shall keep record books and record in them where and when conciliation meetings are held, the name of the conciliation and mediation officer and the parties of their representatives present (Article 36 of the TUI Act). Mention shall be made in the records of documents submitted and the principal proceedings at the meeting. Furthermore, the SCMO shall send the Minister of Welfare reports on his work as often as necessary but never less frequently than once a year.

### I. Compromise Proposal

*416.* If the SCMO's attempts at conciliation prove fruitless, he may submit a compromise proposal to resolve an industrial dispute (Article 27 of the TUI Act). The SCMO consults the parties' negotiating committees and then submits such a proposal for approval or rejection, to the employees' trade unions or federations of trade unions and employers, or an individual employer if only one employer is involved in the industrial dispute. If the dispute in question only concerns a specific union division, an occupation within a union or a union federation, or a specific enterprise, a conciliation and mediation officer may decide that only that division, occupation or enterprise shall be involved in the ballot.

*417.* When two or more unions or union federations are involved in a dispute, a conciliation and mediation officer may, in consultation with the negotiation committees, submit a compromise proposal which applies to more than one party to the dispute, or to all of them (Article 28 of the TUI Act). The same provision furthermore provides for conditions for a conciliation and mediation officer being able to submit one or more compromise proposals which are as follows:

– that negotiation has taken place on the demands that have been presented, including special matters, or that fruitless attempts have been made to hold negotiations according to the negotiation schedule;
– that the time allocated under the negotiation schedule for negotiations between the parties without the mediation of a conciliation and mediation officer has run out without an agreement having been reached;
– that a conciliation and mediation officer has sought to conciliate all the contracting parties involved and considers that there is no prospect for a settlement between them;
– that the collective agreements have been open for review for some time so that the contracting parties have had an opportunity to press for accession to their demands;
– that the parties to the industrial dispute have had the opportunity to express their comments on the conciliation and mediation officer's ideas of making a joint compromise proposal, this idea having been made known to them directly or publicly.

*418.* The SCMO may present compromise proposals as often as he considers necessary to resolve the dispute at hand. Furthermore, if either of the parties wishes to approve a conciliation and mediation officer's compromise proposal after attempts at conciliation have been discontinued without result, a declaration to that effect shall be sent to the conciliation and mediation officer who should immediately inform the opposite party in the dispute of the declaration. If the opposite party also wishes to approve the compromise proposal, the conciliation and mediation officer shall arrange for the parties to conclude the agreement between themselves.

## II. Rules of Voting

*419.* The parties to an industrial dispute shall ensure that their members who have the right to vote are able to acquaint themselves with the compromise proposal as a whole (Article 29 of the TUI Act). Parties to an industrial dispute can make an extract from a compromise proposal for its members in consultation with the conciliation and mediation officer may, who also can after consulting the parties, extract the main points of a compromise proposal in order to make it easy for the members of the disputing parties to acquaint themselves with its contents and to adopt an informed position on the proposal and its effect on their interests. A compromise proposal may not be made known to parties other than those involved without the approval of the conciliation and mediation officer until it has been put to a ballot. A compromise proposal is to be put to the vote in a ballot involving all the parties with the right to vote in the form in which it is presented by the conciliation and mediation officer, where it shall be approved or rejected. In cases of joint proposals, voting and the counting of votes are to take place jointly in all the unions or federations to which the compromise proposal applies so that the combined number of votes will determine whether the proposal is approved or rejected. A conciliation and mediation officer may also organize a joint ballot, even in cases where he makes more than one compromise proposal, providing this is done at the same time.

*420.*  Voting on a compromise proposal shall take place at a ballot meeting which shall last for a previously determined length of time (Article 29 of the TUI Act). The SCMO may, in consultation with the parties, decide that voting shall also take place at specific places or in specific areas outside the ballot meeting. Instead of voting at and outside a ballot meeting, the SCMO can furthermore decide in consultation with the parties, that voting on a compromise proposal is to take place in the form of a secret postal ballot among the union members, which shall be completed within a previously determined period. After consulting with the parties of an industrial dispute, the SCMO shall give further instructions on the conduct of the ballot, e.g., concerning when and how it is to be held.

*421.*  Voting on a compromise proposal shall always be secret and in writing. The votes and ballot materials shall be delivered to the conciliation and mediation officer as soon as voting is complete (Article 30 of the TUI Act). The counting of the votes shall take place under the direction of the conciliation and mediation officer, but each party to the proposal may have a representative present at the counting. A compromise proposal shall be regarded as having been rejected in a ballot if more than half the votes cast are against it and if the votes against it amount to more than one-quarter of the votes according to the voting roll or members' register. This applies equally to ballots conducted at a ballot meeting and postal ballots.

§4. Arbitration

*422.*  There are examples of collective agreements and special agreements between parties on the labour market including provisions regarding disputes being referred to an arbitration tribunal. Such a provision can for example be found in an agreement by the Confederation of Icelandic Bank and Finance Employees, where it is stated that in cases of disputes lasting longer than thirty days the negotiating parties can refer the dispute to an arbitration tribunal, composed of one member from each party and a chairman which the parties agree upon. The chairman then appoints to additional members to the tribunal. However, even though such provisions exist, they are generally not utilized in the Icelandic labour market. In practice, cases of disputes regarding interpretation and legitimate of collective agreement provisions have virtually without exception been referred to the Labour Court.

## §5. INTERACTION AND ROLE OF THE GOVERNMENT

*423.* The Icelandic labour legislation does not provide a role for authorities in industrial disputes other than to facilitate settlements; a role which is performed by the SCMO. It has, however, become increasingly common for the government to take part in the solution of disputes by introducing particular measures in the political arena to accommodate the demands of the labour market. Such government measures are usually referred to as 'social packages', and the chief areas that have been covered by these measures are social issues of various kinds, such as the welfare of the elderly and the disabled, housing policy, unemployment insurance, safety in the workplace, pensions and taxation. Numerous important pieces of legislation in the area of public welfare can be traced back to these social packages. Furthermore, since the 1990 National Social Pact the labour market parties have taken an increasing initiative in controlling inflation through restraint in agreements, in close cooperation with authorities. Promises on behalf of the Government to facilitate settlements have generally involved major changes in economic and fiscal matters, e.g., through reductions in import duties and the pricing of various public services. Through this government interaction a tradition of trilateral cooperation has formed on the Icelandic labour market in the last decades which has led to more stability and reduced the severity of industrial disputes.

*424.* As previously covered in paragraphs 389–394, the government can intervene by passing legislation banning industrial action on the grounds of economic justifications or severe public interests. When it comes to the protection of vital needs, the CAPS Act furthermore stipulates that certain categories of public servants are banned from participating in industrial action in addition to authorizing authorities to call employees who are participating in a legal work stoppage, back to work temporarily in order to prevent crises.

# Selected Bibliography

Adalsteinsson, G.D. (2006). Verkföll og verkfallstíðni á íslenskum vinnumarkaðði 1976–2004 (Work Stoppages and Statistics on the Icelandic Labour Market 1976–2004). *Stjórnmál og stjórnsýsla*, 2, 175–196.

Adalsteinsson, G.D. (2008). Vinnulöggjöfin (lög nr. 80/1938) í 70 ár (The Labour Market Legislation (Act no. 80/1938) for 70 Years). *Stjórnmál og stjórnsýsla*, 4, 181–204.

Adalsteinsson, G.D. and Fridriksson, F. (2010). Lög á verkföll á Íslandi 1985–2010: Um forsendur lagasetningar (Legislation Intervening Strikes in Iceland 1985–2010: Grounds for Such Action). *Stjórnmál og stjórnsýsla*, 6, 151–183.

Althýdusamband, Í. (2010). *Icelandic Labour Law, a Summary of Basic Rights and Obligations on the Private Labour Market*. Reykjavík: Althýdusamband Íslands.

Althýdusamband, Í. (ed.). *Labour Law* (Vinnuréttur). Downloaded 10 October 2011 from: http://www.asi.is/desktopdefault.aspx/tabid-101/.

Andrason, Ó.D. (2007). Sveigjanleiki launa á íslenskum vinnumarkadi (The Flexibility of Salaries on the Icelandic Labour Market). Unpublished MS thesis: University of Iceland, Faculty of Business Administration and Economics.

Arnardóttir, O.M. (2009). Vernd gegn mismunun í íslenskum rétti: breytinga er thörf (Protection Against Discrimination under Icelandic Law: Change Is Needed). *Tímarit lögfrædinga*, 59, 51–83.

Björgvinsson, D.T. (2006). *EES-réttur og landsréttur* (*EEA Law and National Law*). Reykjavík: Codex.

Blöndal, E. (2003). Vernd verkfallsréttarins skv. 74. gr. stjórnarskrárinnar: í ljósi althjóðlegra sáttmála og dóms Hæstaréttar Íslands frá 14. nóvember 2002 (Protection of the Right to Strike under Article 74 of the Icelandic Constitution: In the Light of International Conventions and the Supreme Court's Judgement from 14 November 2002). *Tímarit lögfrædinga*, 53, 273–306.

Blöndal, E. (2003). Althjódavinnumálastofnunin og áhrif samthykkta hennar á íslenskan rétt (The International Labour Organization (ILO) and the Implications of Its Conventions on Icelandic Law). In S.M. Stefánsson and V.M. Matthíasson (eds), *Lögberg* (pp. 275–313). Reykjavík: Háskólaútgáfan.

Blöndal, E. (2005). Funda- og félagafrelsi (Freedom of Assembly and Association). In B. Thorarensen, D.T. Björgvinsson, G. Gauksdóttir and H.B. Hákonardóttir (eds), *Mannréttindasáttmáli Evrópu: Meginreglur, framkvæmd og áhrif á íslenskan rétt* (pp. 390–422). Reykjavík: Mannréttindastofnun Háskóla Íslands.

## Selected Bibliography

Blöndal, E. (2016). New Forms of Employment in Iceland. In Blanpain, R. and Hendrickx, F. (eds), *New Forms of Employment in Europe* (pp. 243–247). Alphen aan den Rijn: Kluwer Law International B.V.

Blöndal, E. and Hjaltadóttir, I.B. (2017). The Concept of 'Employee': The Position in Iceland. In Waas, B. and van Voss, G.H. (eds), *Restatement of Labour Law in Europe* (pp. 309–327). Portland, Oregon: Hart Publishing.

Blöndal, E. (2006). The Sørensen and Rasmussen v. Denmark Judgment by the European Court of Human Rights: Implications for Iceland. *Nordisk Journal of Human Rights*, 24, 206–217.

Blöndal, E. (2007). Takmarkanir á samningsrétti opinberra starfsmanna í ljósi stjórnarskrár og althjóthlegra sáttmála (Limitations of the Right of Public Servants to Bargain Collectively – In Light of the Constitution and International Conventions). *Bifrost Journal of Social Science*, 1, 117–127.

European Commission (2008). Iceland. *Employee Representatives in an Enlarged Europe*, vol. 1 (pp. 275–287). Luxembourg: Office for Official Publication of the European Communities.

Gudmundsson, H. (1974). Kjarasamningar (Collective Agreements). *Tímarit Lögfrædinga*, 24, 72–90.

Haraldsson, Á. (2006). Nokkrar athugasemdir um félagafrelsi opinberra starfsmanna (Notes on the Freedom of Association in Regard to Public Servants). In J.H. Hafstein, B. Hlödversdóttir and U.S. Bjarndal (eds), *Bifröst* (pp. 11–26). Háskólinn á Bifröst.

Júlíusdóttir, L.V. (1997). *Réttindi og skyldur á vinnumarkaði (Rights and Obligations on the Labour Market)*. Reykjavík: Althýdusamband Íslands.

Júlíusdóttir, L.V. (1995). *Stéttarfélög og vinnudeilur (Trade Unions and Industrial Disputes)*. Reykjavík: Althýdusamband Íslands.

Júlíusdóttir, L.V. (2002). Icelandic Labour Law. *Stability and Change in Nordic Labour Law*, 43, 358–374.

Júlíusdóttir, L.V. (2008). *Vinnumarkadsréttur (Labour Market Law)*. Script for teaching.

Líndal, S. (1995). Labour Law and Industrial Relationships in Iceland. *The International Journal of Comparative Labour Law and Industrial Relations*, 1995, 112–132.

Lúthersdóttir, A. (2009). *Midstýrd og valddreifd kjarasamningsgerd: fyrirtækjadáttur kjarasamnings (Centralized and Decentralized Collective Agreements: Company-Related Part of a Collective Agreement)*. Unpublished MS thesis: University of Iceland, School of Social Sciences.

Ólafsdóttir, K. (2008). *Er íslenskur vinnumarkadur sveigjanlegur? (Is the Icelandic Labour Market Flexible?)*. Reykjavík: Háskólinn í Reykjavík.

Snævarr, S. (1993). *Haglýsing Íslands (Economic Description of Iceland)*. Reykjavík, Heimskringla, Háskólaforlag Máls og menningar.

Stefánsson, S.M. (2000). *Evrópusambandid og Evrópska efnahagssvædid (The European Union and the European Economic Area)*. Reykjavík: Orator.

Thorarensen, B. (2008). *Stjórnskipunarréttur: Mannréttindi (Constitutional Law: Human Rights)*. Reykjavík, Bókaútgáfan Codex.

# Table of Statutes

The Act on Payment of Wages, No. 28/1930
The Act on Contracts, Agency and Void Legal Instruments, No. 7/1936
The Act on Trade Unions and Industrial Disputes, No. 80/1938
The Constitution of the Republic of Iceland, No. 33/1944
The Act on the Child Support Collection Centre, No. 54/1971
The Act on Collective Agreements in State Owned Banks, No. 34/1977
The Act on Respecting Labourers' Right to Advance Notice of Termination of
    Employment and to Wages on Account of Absence through Illness and Acci-
    dents, No. 19/1979
The Act on Working Environment, Health and Safety in the Workplace, No. 46/1980
The Working Terms and Pension Rights Insurance Act, No. 55/1980
The Act on Seamen, No. 35/1985
The Civil Servants' Collective Agreements Act, No. 94/1986
The Holiday Allowance Act, No. 30/1987
The Act on Withholding Taxes, No. 45/1987
The Act on Contractual Arbitration, No. 53/1989
The Act on Civil Procedure, No. 91/1991
The Act on the Affairs of People with Disabilities, No. 59/1992
The Administrative Procedures Act, No. 37/1993
The Act respecting Private Limited Companies, No. 138/1994
The Act respecting Public Limited Companies, No. 2/1995
The Act on Supervision of Unfair Commercial Practices and Transparency of the
    Market, No. 57/2005
The Act on the Rights and Obligations of Public Servants, No. 70/1996
The Act on Legal Competence, No. 71/1997
The Pension Act, No. 129/1997
The Act on Courts, No. 50/2016
The Local Government Act, No. 138/2011
The Act on European Work Councils, No. 61/1999
The Prohibition on Termination of Employment due to Family Responsibilities Act,
    No. 27/2000
The Collective Redundancies Act, No. 63/2000
The Act on Maternity/Paternity Leave and Parental Leave, No. 95/2000
The Act on the Pay and Conditions of Fishermen, No. 34/2001
The Act on Workers' Rights in the Event of Transfers of Undertakings, No. 72/2002
The Foreign Nationals' Right to Work Act, No. 97/2002

## Table of Statutes

The Children's Act, No. 76/2003
The Wage Guarantee Fund Act, No. 88/2003
The Act on Income Tax No. 90/2003
The Act on Fixed Term Employment, No. 139/2003
The Act on Part-time Workers, No. 10/2004
The Act on the Involvement of Employees in European Companies, No. 27/2004
The Tobacco Control Act, No. 6/2006
The Act on Unemployment Benefits, No. 54/2006
The Act on Labour Market Affairs, No. 55/2006
The Act on Information and Consultation in Undertakings, No. 151/2006
The Act on Crews of Icelandic Fishing boats, Coast Guard Ships and Cruise Ships, No. 30/2007
The Act concerning Involvement of Employees in European Cooperative Societies, No. 44/2007
The Act on Rights and Obligations of Foreign Undertakings that Post Workers Temporarily in Iceland and on their Workers' Terms and Condition of Employment, No. 45/2007
The Social Security Act, No. 100/2007
The Act on Equal Status and Equal Rights of Women and Men, No. 10/2008
The Secondary School Act, No. 92/2008
The Act concerning Involvement of Employees in Cross-border Mergers of Limited Liability Companies, No. 86/2009

Directives

Directive 80/987/EEC
Directive 91/533/EC
Directive 92/85/EC
Directive 94/33/EC
Directive 94/45/EC
Directive 96/34/EC
Directive 96/71/EC
Directive 97/81/EC
Directive 98/59/EC
Directive 1999/70/EC
Directive 2001/23/EC
Directive 2002/14/EC

# Index

*The numbers here refer to paragraph numbers.*

# Index

144

**Index**